THE WANDERING YEARS

LESSONS LEARNED IN THE WILDERNESS
(BOOK 2)

KENNETH A. WINTER

JOIN MY READERS' GROUP FOR UPDATES AND FUTURE RELEASES

Please join my Readers' Group so i can send you a free book, as well as updates and information about future releases in the series.

See the back of the book for details on how to sign up.

* * *

The Wandering Years

Book #2 in the ***Lessons Learned In The Wilderness*** *series.*

Published by:

Kenneth A. Winter

WildernessLessons

Richmond, Virginia

United States of America

kenwinter.org / wildernesslessons.com

Second printing 2015 / Third printing 2018

Cover Design: Melanie Fisher-Wellman

ISBN 978-1-7240790-9-1 (soft cover)

ISBN 978-0-9755897-2-4 (ebook)

Library of Congress Control Number: 2004095500

DEDICATION

* * *

For my life partner, LaVonne, and our children, Justin and Lorél, as we continue to journey by faith together though this wilderness, even when all we can see in all directions is wilderness. For our parents who have encouraged us every step of the way. For Bill Hughes, Robert Smith and Doug Mollo, who have been the men that God has used to give a word aptly spoken at the appropriate time. And for all those family and friends that God has strategically placed in our lives along the way. But most of all, for the honor and glory of the Lord God Jehovah, who is the One who leads us into the wilderness, the One who leads us through the wilderness and the One who – in His time - will lead us out of the wilderness.

* * *

CONTENTS

CHAPTER SCRIPTURE LISTING

* * *

* * *

A WORD OF EXPLANATION

* * *

You will notice that whenever i use the pronoun "I" referring to myself, i have chosen to use a lowercase "i". It is not a typographical error. i know that is contrary to proper English grammar and accepted editorial style guides. i drive editors (and "spell check") crazy by doing this. But years ago the LORD convicted me – personally – that in all things i must decrease and He must increase. And as a way of continuing personal reminder, from that day forward, i have chosen to use a lower case "i" whenever referring to myself. Because of the same conviction, i use a capital letter for any pronoun referring to God. The style guide for the New Living Translation (NLT) does not share that conviction. However, you will see that i have intentionally made that slight revision and capitalized any pronoun referring to God in my quotations of Scripture from the NLT. If i have violated any style guides as a result, please accept my apology, but i must honor this conviction.

Lastly, regarding this matter – this is a <u>personal</u> conviction – and i share it only so that you will understand why i have chosen to deviate from normal editorial practice. i am in no way suggesting or endeavoring to have anyone else subscribe to my conviction. Thanks for your understanding.

* * *

PREFACE

"Now turn around and don't go on toward the land where the Amalekites and Canaanites live. Tomorrow you must set out for the wilderness in the direction of the Red Sea. ...And your children will be like shepherds, wandering in the wilderness forty years."
Numbers 14:25, 33

* * *

Why did a journey that God ordained to take slightly longer than one year, end up taking forty years? Why, instead of enjoying the fruits of the land of milk and honey, did the Israelites end up wandering in the desert wilderness for forty years? Why did one generation follow God out of Egypt only to die there, leaving the next generation to follow Him into the Promised Land? Because their faith fizzled. And like someone once said, "If your faith fizzles before the finish, it was faulty from the first."

When the Israelites left Egypt, they left with their own expectations of what the journey would be like, how it would unfold, and where they would end up. They began their journey with high expectations and great excitement as to how and where God was going to lead them. They didn't really anticipate spending any time in the wilderness, but if they did, it would only be for a short duration. And when things didn't go their way, when things didn't go the way they expected, they complained, they murmured and they disobeyed God. They had lost sight of the fact that God brought them out of Egypt. He orchestrated the circumstances that led to their release from captivity and their exodus from Egypt. God had a purpose and a plan for His people; and it was far beyond the journey or even the Promised Land. He was calling a people unto Himself. He had set this people apart to be His people, a people through whom He would bring salvation to all mankind and a people through whom He would bring glory to His name. The fatal flaw in their faith was that they thought it was all about themselves – their plans, their wants and their desires. Their view of God was that He was their God – in the sense that He was there to fulfill their plans, their wants and their desires. Whereas the reality was that they were His people – and they were on this journey to fulfill His plan, His purpose and His desires.

So every time they hit a bump in the road they would look at it with frustration, anxiety and often, anger. Because the bump didn't fit with their plan. The whole issue came to a head after the twelve spies gave the people their report. The people no longer even wanted to enter the Promised Land. And God knew that if the people couldn't trust Him in the wilderness, there was no way they would be able to trust Him in the Promised Land. So God turned them back to wander.

In my own journeys through the wildernesses of life, i can look back and see where God has turned me back from that land of promise in my life to wander a while longer in the wilderness. God has given us the wilderness to prepare us for His land of promise, but if when we reach the border we are not ready, He will turn us back to wander. But remember, God led the Israelites even as they wandered - and He will lead you as well. This is still a part of His journey for you.

If God is allowing you to wander in the wilderness right now, it is because He has more to teach you about Himself – His Person, His purpose and His power. You have two choices. You can allow Him to teach you all that He desires to teach you and adjust your life to Him; or you can murmur and complain that He has turned you back to wander. The latter, at best, will prolong the wandering, or left unchecked, will cause you to miss the blessing of His land of promise for you. My advice to you is to listen to the "*Lessons Learned In The Wilderness - The Wandering Years*". Remember, God has called you to be used by Him to make a global impact. Allow Him to use these lessons to transform you into that vessel of honor - cleansed and prepared for the Master's use.

Therefore if anyone cleanses himself from the latter, he will be a vessel for honor, sanctified and useful for the Master, prepared for every good work. (2 Tim 2:21 NKJ)

* * *

1

YOU'RE NOT ALONE

One day in midspring, during the second year after Israel's departure from Egypt, the LORD spoke to Moses in the Tabernacle in the wilderness of Sinai. He said, "Take a census of the whole community of Israel by their clans and families. List the names of all the men twenty years old or older who are able to go to war. You and Aaron are to direct the project, assisted by one family leader from each tribe." ...They were counted by families--all the men of Israel who were twenty years old or older and able to go to war. The total number was 603,550.
Numbers 1:1-4, 45-46

* * *

Sometimes as we journey through the wilderness we think that we're all by ourselves. We start to think that there is no one else in the wilderness, and no one else who understands what we are going through.

The census indicated that there were over 600,000 men, able to go to war, aged twenty years and older. Estimating the number of women and children, as well as the tribe of the Levites that were not included in this count, the total number of Israelites easily approached or exceeded two million people, which equals or exceeds the population of ninety-four countries in the world today. This truly was the nation of Israel. This nation was prepared to mobilize an army in excess of 600,000 men if the need arose; that number would only be exceeded by the armies of seven nations in the world today. Are you getting the picture that this was not a small group of people?

. . .

God was now leading His people – His nation – on a journey through the wilderness. He had placed His earthly dwelling place – His tabernacle – in the midst of this people. It was a journey through which God was spreading His Name throughout the world. All who saw or heard about this people were aware that His glorious presence dwelt among and led this people.

A wilderness can be a barren plain or a primeval forest. It can be a place absent of life or brimming with distractions; but a common denominator is always that it is a neglected place without a clear path and not easily traveled. A wilderness is comprised of the unknown and the unusual. A wilderness always begins at the outer edge of that which is familiar. Sometimes the boundary that divides the wilderness from the familiar is obscure; sometimes it is very pointed. Sometimes we are surprised to find that our journey has led us into the wilderness; sometimes we know that we have very deliberately been led to cross that boundary into the wilderness.

The wilderness is a proving ground, a testing place – it is a place where the mettle of which we are made will be tested and proven. Will we be found deficient or will we be found adequate to the test? God led His people – all two million of them - through just such a place for just such a purpose, enroute to His land of promise for them. There they could encourage one another, they could help one another, and, if necessary, they could fight for one another. God wanted to teach the people to trust one another, to depend on one another and to love one another. It was His plan that they be interdependent – that they understand the unique way each of them were gifted. The journey through the wilderness would be accomplished as they learned to journey as a people and not as individuals.

But they could only journey as a people if they were all following the same Leader. That is why sometimes, even when we are in the midst of a crowd, we must come to a place where we are alone. Because it is when we are alone that we will make the personal choice of whom we are going to follow. Will we follow ourselves or the crowd or the Leader? If we are going to follow the leader we must know and understand Who the Leader is. Moses was not the leader; he was the undershepherd. God was the Leader of His people – and He still is. If you have found yourself on a journey through the wilderness, take heart, God is your Leader. And He will not only lead you through the wilderness; He designed the wilderness, so that through it, His purpose can be accomplished. He knows every peak, every valley, and every obstacle ahead. He will use it to test and to prove you. He will use it to spread His Name. He will use it to allow His glorious presence to be seen.

Take heart, you are not alone on this journey. He has placed many of His children on the journey with you. They are here to encourage you and help you, just as you are here to encourage and help them. We are interdependent with one another. Watch for His other children – they are all around you. But also, you are not alone, because your Lord is leading you and He has promised to never leave you or forsake you (Heb 13:5). Follow your Leader – He will lead you through this wilderness.

* * *

2

HAVE YOU BEEN CALLED TO STAND GUARD?

But this total did not include the Levites. For the LORD had said to Moses, "Exempt the tribe of Levi from the census; do not include them when you count the rest of the Israelites. You must put the Levites in charge of the Tabernacle of the Covenant, along with its furnishings and equipment. They must carry the Tabernacle and its equipment as you travel, and they must care for it and camp around it. Whenever the Tabernacle is moved, the Levites will take it down and set it up again. Anyone else who goes too near the Tabernacle will be executed. Each tribe of Israel will have a designated camping area with its own family banner. But the Levites will camp around the Tabernacle of the Covenant to offer the people of Israel protection from the LORD's fierce anger. The Levites are responsible to stand guard around the Tabernacle."

Numbers 1:47-53

* * *

God called the Levites to be in charge of the Tabernacle, and all of its furnishings and equipment. He called them to stand guard and protect it. God dwelt in the midst of His people, but the area immediately surrounding His dwelling place was the home of the Levites. Whenever the pillar of cloud moved from the Tabernacle to lead the people, the Levites took down the Tabernacle and carried it. Whenever the cloud stopped, the Levites would set up the Tabernacle and prepare it for the indwelling presence of God's Spirit.

The Levites were chosen by God and called to this role because of their response after the people had worshiped the image of the golden calf. You may recall that Moses stood at the gate of the camp and said, *"All of you who are on the LORD's side, come over here and join me"* (Ex 32:26). And all of the Levites came to him. He had then instructed them to strap on their swords and kill those who had been responsible for this abomination. Now, lest there be any confusion, the Levites had probably taken part in worshiping the golden calf. Aaron, who had formed the golden calf, was a son of the tribe of Levi. They had been as much a part, if not even more responsible, for the sin of the people. What differentiated them on that day, and as a result, for every day thereafter, was their immediate repentance before the Lord. They recognized their sin, they repented of their sin, and they immediately responded in obedience to the Lord.

Scripture records that the Levites killed 3,000 of their tribe that day, including family members and friends. i believe that left them with a memory that they would never be able to forget and a stain of blood on their hands that they would never be able to wash away. Because they were God's instruments of death, they saw God's wrath poured out upon His rebellious people firsthand. They saw the payment of the wages of sin. With this reminder imbedded in their memories, they understood their charge by God to now protect the people of Israel from the LORD's wrath. They took seriously this charge to protect not only the tabernacle, but also the people, that they might not do anything again that would incite the LORD's wrath.

All of the tribes displayed their family banners in their designated camping area, except the Levites. On that day when Moses had told them, *"Today you have been ordained for the service of the LORD, for you obeyed him even though it meant killing your own sons and brothers. Because of this, he will now give you a great blessing"* (Ex 32:29); and from that day forward Jehovah Nissi was <u>their</u> banner. They had need of no other. His dwelling place was in their midst and He alone was their banner.

In that calling, the Levites served their Lord and they served the people; they stood guard so that nothing would disrupt the Lord's dwelling place and nothing would disrupt Him from dwelling among the people.

The Levites are a picture for us of what Paul was describing when he wrote, *"We are Christ's ambassadors, and God is using us to speak to you. We urge you, as though Christ himself were here pleading with you, 'Be reconciled to*

God!'" (2 Cor 5:20) We have been called to be Christ's ambassadors; we have been called to stand guard. We have been called to communicate His Good News of reconciliation. We are His earthly dwelling place. We have been ordained to this place of service, not because of our goodness but because of His grace. If we have repented of our sin and turned to Him in obedience, He has blessed us with His presence. He has become our banner. Just as the Levites and the Tabernacle became inseparable, so His presence must be equally conspicuous in our lives. He has called us to be His salt and His light. He has called us to be His ambassadors to a people that so desperately need Him. He has called us to stand guard.

* * *

3

ASSIGNED FOR HIS PURPOSE

Then the LORD gave these instructions to Moses and Aaron: "Each tribe will be assigned its own area in the camp, and the various groups will camp beneath their family banners. The Tabernacle will be located at the center of these tribal compounds.... The divisions of Judah, Issachar, and Zebulun are to camp toward the sunrise on the east side of the Tabernacle, beneath their family banners.... These three tribes are to lead the way whenever the Israelites travel to a new campsite. The divisions of Reuben, Simeon, and Gad are to camp on the south side of the Tabernacle, beneath their family banners.... These three tribes will be second in line whenever the Israelites travel. Then the Levites will set out from the middle of the camp with the Tabernacle. All the tribes are to travel in the same order that they camp, each in position under the appropriate family banner. The divisions of Ephraim, Manasseh, and Benjamin are to camp on the west side of the Tabernacle, beneath their family banners... and they will follow the Levites in the line of march. The divisions of Dan, Asher, and Naphtali are to camp on the north side of the Tabernacle, beneath their family banners.... They are to bring up the rear whenever the Israelites move to a new campsite." So the people of Israel did everything just as the LORD had commanded Moses. Each clan and family set up camp and marched under their banners exactly as the LORD had instructed them.
Numbers 2:1-3, 9-10, 16-18, 24-25, 31, 34

* * *

Did you ever stop and think about all of the logistics involved in moving a group of two million people from Egypt to the Promised Land? i am mindful of all of the planning that goes into a trip for my wife, two children and me. i am also mindful of the occasional disagreement that arises over who sits where, who sleeps where, who gets to go first, etc. Now imagine doing that with two million people! God was leading His people on a journey through the wilderness and He would leave no detail unresolved.

In their journey through the wilderness, as well as in ours, it is God who makes the assignments. He assigns our places. Can you imagine the quarreling that would have taken place between the people if it had been left to them to determine who camped where in relation to the Tabernacle? Or imagine the infighting that would have taken place over which clan and tribe got to lead out in the journey. Also, notice that God did not delegate the assignment to Moses. God knew the grief the people would give him if he chose the order, so God Himself made the assignment.

He appointed their positions. God named the captains of each tribe. He alone equips, empowers and enables each of us for the position to which He appoints us. Our God is a God of order; and there is much to be learned by looking at the order of His assignments of the tribes.

As we look at their assignments, i want you to see that their pedigree determined their place - their position to their father Jacob was a factor in their placement. Our placement will also be determined by our position and relationship to our Heavenly Father through Jesus Christ. Our effectiveness in the wilderness, as well as in the Promised Land, will be directly proportional to our proximity to the Father – the closer we are to Him, the more effective we will be. Secondly, God's purpose dictated their position. They were assigned not only based upon their parentage but also their giftedness.

The Lord took the tribes, with the exception of the Levites, and divided them into four groups of three tribes. The first group was led by the tribe of Judah. This group camped on the east side of the tabernacle, toward the rising sun. It was appropriate that this group be first, and that they be led by the tribe of Judah. The tribe of Judah was the largest tribe with the largest contingent of fighting men. Their namesake, Judah, though not the firstborn of Jacob, was the first to be given a blessing by his father. Jacob gave him a place of preeminence over his brothers (Gen 49:8). The very name "Judah" means "praise the Lord". Their position in leadership evidenced the preeminence of praise as they, and we, journey across the wilderness. The Lord God Jehovah is worthy of and due praise above all else and before all else. The tribe of Judah was the tribe from which Christ would come, He who is First and Last, Beginning and End. The very captain named by God to lead the tribe of Judah is Nahson, an ancestor of our Lord and listed in His ancestry in Matthew 1:4. Issachar and Zebulun were Judah's two younger brothers, all being sons of Leah. As these tribes led the people, their very names indicated that God indwells the praises of His people and He is a Rewarder of those who praise Him.

The second group camped on the south side of the Tabernacle and was led by the tribe of Reuben, the firstborn of Jacob. Reuben and Simeon, the second-born of Jacob, together with Gad, came before the tribe of Levi, the third-born of Jacob. Their names and position indicated that as they walked before the Lord, He would look upon them, He would hear them and He would bless them. Though their blessing had been given to Judah, their birthright as sons of Jacob had earned them this position before the Tabernacle. As we walk in obedience before our Lord we too will experience His blessing; but like this second group, our position to the Lord is unmerited favor through Jesus Christ – it is our birthright through Jesus – a birthright of grace and not of our works, "lest any of us have anything to boast about".

As we have already seen, the Levites encamped around the Tabernacle and carried it between the second and third groups when the Israelites traveled. This position reflected Jehovah's indwelling presence in the midst of His people.

The third group camped on the west side of the Tabernacle. These were the sons of Rachel, the favored sons of Jacob. These were led by the tribe of Ephraim. Ephraim, though the second-born of Joseph, was blessed before and above his brother, Manasseh, by their grandfather Jacob (Gen. 48:17-19). As a result of that blessing, this tribe led this group. Their very names spoke of the Father's love and blessing, even in the midst of trouble. As they journeyed in pursuit of the dwelling place of the Lord, walking in His shadow, they were constantly reminded, as well as they were a constant reminder, of the Father's goodness and compassion.

The fourth group camped on the north side of the Tabernacle and was led by the tribe of Dan; the eldest son of Jacob by Rachel's maidservant, Bilhah. The military prowess and feats of the tribe of Dan was celebrated throughout their recorded history. This, together with the size of their fighting force, made them an appropriate choice for this last group. They, together with the tribes of Naphtali and Asher, the remaining sons of the maidservants, became the rearguard. Their names indicated that they had been judged by their Lord and had been vindicated; they had prevailed and been blessed. They were a fitting conclusion to the testimony of the grace and the mercy of their Lord as the Israelites journeyed through the wilderness.

We should see one more aspect of this assemblage. Each of the four groups carried a banner. The banner was for identification; and it served as a rallying point for the people. According to rabbinical tradition, each banner carried an emblem that represented that tribe. The first group led by the tribe of Judah, bore the likeness of a lion; the second led by the tribe of Reuben, bore the likeness of a man; the third led by the tribe of Ephraim, bore the likeness of an ox; and the fourth led by the tribe of Dan, bore the likeness of an eagle. And in the midst of these four emblems was the Wilderness Tabernacle, the earthly dwelling place of the Spirit of God. In Revelation 4:6-8, we read, *"In front of the throne was a shiny sea of glass, sparkling like crystal. In the center and around the throne were four living beings, each covered with eyes, front and back. The first of these living beings had the form of a lion; the second looked like an ox; the third had a human face; and the fourth had the form of an eagle with wings spread out as though in flight. Each of these living beings had six wings, and their wings were covered with eyes, inside and out. Day after day and night after night they keep on saying, 'Holy, holy, holy is the Lord God Almighty--the one who always was, who is, and who is still to come.'"* As the Israelites camped and journeyed in the wilderness, they were a picture to us, even now, of this expression of worship in heaven of the Lord God Jehovah recorded by John. Every aspect of their journey, including the emblem on their banners, was a picture and an expression of worship.

God desires for every facet of our journey to be an expression of worship to Him. He has placed us according to our pedigree in Him, and He has positioned us in accordance with His purpose. Be faithful in the assignment He has given you; it is not about us – it is all about Him!

* * *

4

CONSECRATED TO SERVE

This is the family line of Aaron and Moses as it was recorded when the LORD spoke to Moses on Mount Sinai: Aaron's sons were Nadab (the firstborn), Abihu, Eleazar, and Ithamar. They were anointed and set apart to minister as priests. But Nadab and Abihu died in the LORD's presence in the wilderness of Sinai when they burned before the LORD a different kind of fire than he had commanded. Since they had no sons, this left only Eleazar and Ithamar to serve as priests with their father, Aaron.

Numbers 3:1-4

* * *

Aaron and his eldest sons Nadab and Abihu, together with seventy of the elders of Israel, climbed partway up Mount Sinai with Moses (Ex 24:9). There they saw the God of Israel and shared a meal together in His presence. Having seen God, they were now being given an opportunity to serve Him as doorkeepers in His House.

Aaron and all four of his sons were chosen by God to serve Him and intercede for the people as High Priests. God gave them very specific instructions on how offerings were to be presented before Him. He left nothing to their imagination or their intellect. He knew that an unholy people could not conceive or comprehend of how to worship a holy God. God directed Moses to consecrate Aaron and his sons to their priestly service through the ceremonial washing with water, the robing in their priestly vestments, the sprinkling of sacrificial blood, and the anointing with oil (Leviticus 8).

• • •

The washing with water signified the cleansing that must take place in the priests lives before they could serve the Lord. They must be holy and pure before they could enter into His presence. The same is true of us. We have been chosen by God to serve Him. We can only enter into that service through salvation through Jesus Christ – apart from Him we can do absolutely nothing. But before we can be used, we too must be cleansed of unconfessed sins and impurities in our lives. Jesus taught this very principle to His disciples in the upper room that night before He was arrested, when He washed His disciples' feet. But as He explained to Peter, because of their relationship with Him, they did not need to be washed all over; only their feet needed to be washed. By doing so, they would be prepared for service and prepared to enter into fellowship with Him. Moses washed Aaron and his sons in the same manner that Jesus washed the disciples' feet.

Next, Moses clothed them in their priestly garments. The clothing was made of white linen signifying the righteousness of God. As they served Him and entered into His presence, they could only do so clothed in His righteousness – just as we, as followers of Jesus, can only enter into God's presence clothed in the righteousness of Christ.

Then Moses applied some of the droplets of blood of the sacrifice to their right ear lobe, right thumb, and right big toe. This represents for us that only through the shed blood of the perfect Sacrifice, Jesus, can we hear the voice of God, be fit as His hands in service, and be prepared to walk with Him. It symbolized that our total personality is cleansed by Christ's blood and must therefore be presented to Him as an act of worship (Rom 12:1-2).

Lastly, Moses anointed the priests with oil. In the case of Aaron, this involved pouring the oil on his head and allowing it to drip down over his beard and his clothing. This represented the anointing of the Holy Spirit and symbolizes that He is free to move and to work in our worship and service.

But just as God had consecrated them for His purpose, His consecration led them to greater accountability before Him, and greater consequence for disobedience. **God's anointing is His empowerment to the obedient; it is not His shelter to the disobedient.** God is a jealous God. He will not be mocked. And He can only be approached in one way – His Way. Just as all roads don't lead to a relationship with the Holy God, all roads are not acceptable to Him in worship and in service. God gave His high priests very specific instructions on how they were to serve Him and worship Him in the tabernacle. Nadab (meaning "spontaneous") and Abihu (meaning "worshipper of God") made the decision to spontaneously worship God in an unauthorized way – a way contrary to that which God commanded – and the consequence was death. God will not ignore disobedience – even the disobedience of His anointed children.

But God will accomplish His purpose – His purpose will continue. Though Nadab and Abihu had no children to follow them as high priests, they did have two younger brothers, Eleazar and Ithamar. God had chosen them, He had prepared them, He had consecrated them and now He placed them in service. God will always accomplish His work and His purpose – nothing will prevent Him from accomplishing His appointed task, including our disobedience. At the very least, our disobedience will render us ineffective and therefore unable to experience the blessing of being used by God. In other instances, like these young men, our disobedience could render us permanently disqualified from service. But, in either case, the sovereign and almighty God will not be thwarted in His purpose.

Even in the midst of your journey, God has called you and consecrated you to worship Him and serve Him. Listen carefully, heed His instruction and experience His blessing as you worship and serve the Lord God Jehovah.

* * *

5

A BLESSING IN THE WILDERNESS

Then the LORD said to Moses,
"Instruct Aaron and his sons to bless the people of Israel with this special blessing:
'May the LORD bless you and protect you.
May the LORD smile on you and be gracious to you.
May the LORD show you his favor and give you his peace.'
This is how Aaron and his sons will designate the Israelites as my people, and I myself will bless them."
Numbers 6:22-27

* * *

Journeying through the wilderness can make you weary. The Israelites had been on their journey for approximately one year now; and though they had experienced God's provision and protection, they were ready for the journey to be over. When you're on a journey like that there is no place to really call home – whatever there was, is no more because you've left it behind; and whatever is ahead, you have yet to experience. You feel displaced. You tend to feel disconnected from the world around you. (That's partly why God leads us on journeys like this, to disconnect us from those things that would otherwise distract us from Him and what He wants to teach us.) But even knowing that, there can be a disquieting in your spirit. As i write this, my family and i are nearing the fourth month of a similar journey; and though we count this time precious and thank our Lord for His faithfulness, i would not be completely truthful if i didn't tell you, we're ready for the journey to be over! We didn't expect the journey to take this long. We expected to arrive in God's Land of Promise for us a long time ago. We hunger to put down roots in that new land. As grateful as we are for God's provision and His protection, we're ready for the journey to be over. We're ready to share the testimony of what God did through the journey, instead of what He is doing.

So, i'm thinking, that is about what the Israelites were thinking when God told Moses to instruct Aaron and his sons to bless the people. And what a blessing it was!

May the Lord bless you and protect you. We are admonished by the psalmist to bless God. *"Bless the LORD, O my soul; and all that is within me, bless His holy name! Bless the LORD, O my soul, and forget not all His benefits"* (Ps 103:1-2 – NKJ). We are to acknowledge Him for Who He is and thank Him for all that He has done. We are to bless one another, expressing our wishes for God's blessing on one another's behalf. But when God blesses us, that is wholly another matter! What we say, we hope will come to fruition; what God says, He will move heaven and earth to bring about. What He wills, He does; and what He does, He completes. As the sovereign and almighty God, when God blesses us, He does so with His best for us in mind. As the omnipresent and omniscient God, when He blesses us, He does so in ways that are not only for time but also for eternity. And God's blessings will exceed anything that we can imagine, because His view is far greater than ours. His blessing will include His protection – protection from anything or anyone under His Lordship – and that includes anything or anybody, including Satan and his minions. Can you think of anything greater than a blessing from the Creator of the universe? How about from your Heavenly Father who loves you perfectly? How about from the King of kings and the Lord of lords? May He bless you with His blessing and His protection!

May the Lord smile on you and be gracious to you. i can think of nothing more inviting, nothing more comforting and nothing more encouraging than the Lord's smile. It is a smile that at once communicates His love, His acceptance, His concern, His compassion, His delight, His tenderness and His welcome. It is a smile that includes; it doesn't exclude. It is a smile that encourages; it doesn't ridicule. It is a smile that says, "I love you more than you will ever know." And with it is a grace and a graciousness that cost Him the shed blood of His Son. It is a grace and a graciousness that gives and gives and gives, when i have done absolutely nothing to merit it. When i didn't love Him, He was gracious. When i didn't obey Him, He was gracious. When i ignored Him, He was gracious. May He smile upon you and may you grasp and comprehend the full extent of His grace and His graciousness!

May the Lord show you His favor and give you His peace. His favor includes His kindness and His goodness, but it is more than that. It includes His support and His friendship, but it is more than that. It includes His mildness and His mercy, but it is more than that. His favor is He extending to me and on my behalf all that is His; placing all that is His at my disposal for my benefit. And with that favor He extends His peace – His peace that exceeds all understanding - a peace that comforts in the midst of any circumstance, and a peace that calms any storm. May you experience the fullness of His favor and the depths of His peace!

Fellow sojourner, take heart, no matter how much longer your journey is or where you are in the wilderness:

> *'May the LORD bless you and protect you.*
> *May the LORD smile on you and be gracious to you.*
> *May the LORD show you His favor and give you His peace.'*

* * *

6

WHY ISN'T THE CLOUD MOVING?

The Tabernacle was set up, and on that day the cloud covered it. Then from evening until morning the cloud over the Tabernacle appeared to be a pillar of fire.... When the cloud lifted from over the sacred tent, the people of Israel followed it. And wherever the cloud settled, the people of Israel camped. In this way, they traveled at the LORD's command and stopped wherever he told them to.... Whether the cloud stayed above the Tabernacle for two days, a month, or a year, the people of Israel stayed in camp and did not move on. But as soon as it lifted, they broke camp and moved on. So they camped or traveled at the LORD's command, and they did whatever the LORD told them through Moses.
Numbers 9:15, 17-18, 22-23

* * *

God was true to His Word. When the Tabernacle was completed, His Spirit covered it as a cloud and dwelt within it. Then, whenever God was ready for the people to move on, the cloud would lift and go before them. But as long as the cloud covered the Tabernacle, the Israelites would stay in camp and not move on. Sometimes they would encamp overnight. Sometimes they would encamp by day and follow the fiery pillar through the hours of night. Sometimes they would encamp for days, for weeks or for months at a time. The people didn't determine when it was time to go. The priests didn't determine when it was time to go. Moses didn't determine when it was time to go. Only God determined the time; and when He was ready, His Spirit led them. Sometimes they moved with haste ("I, the Lord, will hasten it in its time" – Isa 60:22 NKJ), but sometimes they didn't move at all. Lookouts kept their eyes trained on the cloud. "Is today a camping day or a traveling day?" "Do we break camp today and follow in His path, or do we remain and wait in His presence?" On the days that the cloud lifted, the cry would go forth, "Break camp, we are leaving!" On other days there would be silence as they waited.

If you have journeyed through the wilderness following God's pillar of cloud, you, too, have experienced the uncertainty of the waiting. I can hear the children of the Israelites asking their parents, "Why can't we go now? Why must we wait so long?" i can hear the adults, as they peered up into the sky, asking the priests, "Why isn't the cloud moving?" i can hear Aaron asking Moses, "What is God waiting for?" God had promised to deliver them into the land of His promise; why must they now tarry in the wilderness?

Today i feel just like that. "Lord, why do You tarry in this place? Shouldn't we leave just now?" But as i ask these questions, i am reminded of another time when followers of our Lord, sons of Israel, asked the same question. Jesus had just gotten news that His dear friend Lazarus was sick unto death. His sisters, Martha and Mary, knew that if Jesus came He could heal Lazarus. Time was of the essence; they must leave now and travel with haste to Bethany. But Jesus remained where He was for two days. Now if you or i were there we probably would have said, "Master, I don't think you understand. We must leave now. He whom You love is sick." And i can just imagine Jesus looking back at us with that patient, all-knowing and understanding smile that said, "You don't get this, but you will. Be patient. Everything is as the Father planned. All will be for the glory of God." Days later, Jesus looked at Martha and said, *"You will see God's glory if you believe"* (John 11:40). And moments later, Lazarus, "who had died came forth" from the grave. Jesus' delay had been a part of the plan – the plan of God's glory. Jesus understood that His entire purpose was to bring glory to the Father – every act, every action, every word, every step, … and every stop – was about God's glory.

As you tarry at your encampment, remember this truth: **every step and every stop is about God's glory**. He has placed you on this journey for His glory. He alone knows best how that will be brought about. He is God over the details and the delays. He is God when His pillar of cloud leads you to go and when it covers you to stay. *"'My thoughts are completely different from yours,' says the LORD. 'And my ways are far beyond anything you could imagine. For just as the heavens are higher than the earth, so are my ways higher than your ways and my thoughts higher than your thoughts'"* (Isa 55:8-9).

As you tarry, remember **God is working in your life even now to prepare you for what He is preparing for you up ahead**. In His sovereign timing, He will bring those two points into intersection. And when He does, "you will see God's glory if you believe." In the meantime, keep your eye on His pillar of cloud. And as long as the cloud isn't moving, wait with Him. Trust Him, the cry to "break camp" will come. When everything is ready, He will move; and you will see God's glory.

* * *

7

TWO TRUMPETS

Now the LORD said to Moses, "Make two trumpets of beaten silver to be used for summoning the people to assemble and for signaling the breaking of camp… You must sound short blasts to signal moving on. But when you call the people to an assembly, blow the trumpets using a different signal… When you arrive in your own land and go to war against your enemies, you must sound the alarm with these trumpets so the LORD your God will remember you and rescue you from your enemies. Blow the trumpets in times of gladness, too, sounding them at your annual festivals and at the beginning of each month to rejoice over your burnt offerings and peace offerings. The trumpets will remind the LORD your God of his covenant with you. I am the LORD your God."

Numbers 10:1-2, 6-7, 9-10

* * *

In my younger days, i was a trumpet player. i enjoyed its versatility – the trumpet was an instrument that could be used to play a wide diversity of musical styles from classical to contemporary, from fanfare to farewell, and from melodic to harmonic. It is an instrument that is as much at home on the battlefield as it is at the pep rally, in the concert hall as it is in the cathedral, and in the wedding procession as it is on the burial ground. It has been used to sound the charge as well as the retreat, the joy of victory as well as the mourning of defeat, and the celebration as well as the commemoration.

And on this day in the wilderness, the Lord said to Moses, "Make two trumpets of beaten silver." The trumpets were to be used for summoning and signaling, as an alarm and a reminder, as an announcement of celebratory gladness and reverent rejoicing. But most of all the trumpets were to serve as a reminder to the Lord of His covenant with the people. It is interesting to me that these trumpets were forged and formed in the wilderness. They were not brought from Egypt. They would have purpose in the wilderness but they would have even greater purpose in the Promised Land.

There is greater value in instruments formed in the wilderness. Instruments formed in the wilderness are more durable; they take more of a beating. The journey and the conditions are such that the instrument isn't pampered; it must endure greater hardship. But that hardship results in a heartier instrument – one with greater strength and stamina.

God chose to have the trumpets made out of silver. Silver is strong; it will hold its shape. It is ductile; it can be elongated and stretched beyond its original confines. It is malleable; it can be molded and shaped into any form. It can endure extreme temperature changes. The maker will use extreme heat to remove any impurities, or dross, in the silver. And as the dross is removed, the instrument will take on an attractive shiny appearance, a finish that reflects radiated light and reflects the image of its maker. The purer the silver is made, the clearer the reflected image becomes. It is interesting to note that when all of the impurities are removed, silver does not radiate its own image, it purely reflects the image of he who made it, and those around it. Silver also gave the trumpet a richer and more resonant sound over other metals. It gave it a "voice" that was distinctly different and sounded with a superior consonance when used by the instrument's player or maker.

God is making His instruments in your journey as well. He is forming His trumpet – you – for His purpose. This instrument will have greater value having been formed in the wilderness as well. The Maker is molding you and shaping you for just His purpose. The stress that He uses in the process will be sufficient to bend you without breaking you. (He may bring you to a place of brokenness – a complete dependence upon Him – but He will not leave you in pieces.) The heat He uses will be sufficient to remove all of the dross without scalding the silver. He will leave no blemish, though He will probably leave His fingerprints. God has led you on this journey of faith through the wilderness, and part of His purpose is to form you into just such an instrument – an instrument formed by the

Master and forged through faith. James writes, "*For when your faith is tested, your endurance has a chance to grow. So let it grow, for when your endurance is fully developed, you will be strong in character and ready for anything*" (James 1:3-4).

Yes, God will use you as His instrument in the wilderness, but more than that, He is preparing you for His use in His land of promise. And His handiwork will be a reminder to Him of His covenant with you – He is your God and you are His trumpet; His trumpet formed and forged in the wilderness.

* * *

8

ON TO PARAN

One day in midspring, during the second year after Israel's departure from Egypt, the cloud lifted from the Tabernacle of the Covenant. So the Israelites set out from the wilderness of Sinai and traveled on in stages until the cloud stopped in the wilderness of Paran.... They marched for three days after leaving the mountain of the LORD, with the Ark of the LORD's covenant moving ahead of them to show them where to stop and rest. As they moved on each day, the cloud of the LORD hovered over them. And whenever the Ark set out, Moses would cry, "Arise, O LORD, and let your enemies be scattered! Let them flee before you!" And when the Ark was set down, he would say, "Return, O LORD, to the countless thousands of Israel!"

Numbers 10:11-12, 33-36

* * *

After having camped at Mount Sinai for almost a year, the cloud lifted and the people were on their way. It would be a three-day journey to the wilderness of Paran. (The wilderness of Paran is where Hagar and Ishmael found refuge when Sarah had Abraham send them away.) The wilderness of Paran was bounded on the north by southern Canaan, the Promised Land. They were in the fourteenth month of their journey and they were now that close to the Promised Land!

The people that left Sinai were much different from the people who had arrived a year earlier. They arrived as a ragtag multitude following the promises of God; they left as an ordered people following the presence of

God. Prior to Sinai they had experienced God's provision and protection, but at Sinai they experienced His Person and His presence dwelling in their midst. They arrived in Sinai with a self-centered view of God, His promises and His purpose. They left Sinai as the recipients of His Law and His covenant, with a better understanding of His purpose and His plan for their lives. The Israelites left Sinai, not only having experienced God's presence, but also having experienced His wrath and His judgment following their worship of the golden calf. Prior to Sinai they had seen God's power directed against their enemies, but now they had seen God's power directed against them and their disobedience, and they had learned to live in the reverence and awe of the Almighty God.

As they left Sinai, the Mount was behind them, but the Ark of the Lord's covenant was before them. Though the people would never return to the Mount of the Lord; the Lord of the Mount would continue to go before them. The ark, which had been crafted while they were at Sinai, contained the two stone tablets of the Law – God's covenant with His people; as well as the golden pot of manna – a testimony to future generations of God's faithful provision. On the top of the ark was the mercy seat, the place where God spoke to Moses in the Wilderness Tabernacle – the visible symbol of His gracious presence. The Ark represented the Presence and the promises of God that went before His people.

They arrived in Sinai carrying riches from Egypt. While there, God transformed those riches into His Wilderness Tabernacle – the earthly dwelling place of God. The tribe of Levi arrived in Sinai as one of many. They left Sinai having been consecrated as the servants and priests of God.

Picture this: the Ark of God's Covenant goes before them, the Mount of the Lord lies behind them, the Tabernacle of the Lord travels in their midst and the Cloud of the Lord covers them. They arrived in Sinai led by God; they now left encompassed by His presence - shaded, protected and bounded by His limitless power and grace.

Being positioned in such a way in the presence of God gave them a posture of confidence in the power of God. (Unfortunately this confidence would only be short-lived.) But now, as they advanced closer to God's Land of Promise for them, and the ever-closer reality of the enemies that stood before them, they confessed a confidence in the power of God to accomplish His purpose by defeating and scattering those enemies and giving His people rest.

As you journey on to the Paran in your wilderness, you, too, can do so in the awareness that you are encompassed by His presence. You are shaded, protected and bounded by His limitless power and grace. Be confident that He will scatter the enemies before you and He will give you rest.

* * *

9

A BELOVED SON

One day Moses said to his brother-in-law, Hobab son of Reuel the Midianite, "We are on our way to the Promised Land. Come with us and we will treat you well, for the LORD has given wonderful promises to Israel!" But Hobab replied, "No, I will not go. I must return to my own land and family." "Please don't leave us," Moses pleaded. "You know the places in the wilderness where we should camp. Come, be our guide and we will share with you all the good things that the LORD does for us."

Numbers 10:29-32

* * *

Reuel the Midianite is Jethro the priest of Midian, the father of Moses' wife Zipporah. Scholars tell us that Jethro, which means "excellence", was probably his official title, whereas Reuel, which means "friend of God", was probably his proper name. i propose that there may be one other explanation for this difference. You may recall that Jethro arrived at Sinai, bringing Moses' wife and two sons. Not only did he travel to Sinai on this personal mission, he also came in an official capacity, to formally greet the Israelites on behalf of his people the Midianites. While visiting with Moses (Ex 18:12), Jethro declared his personal allegiance to Jehovah. Though he arrived at Sinai as an Excellency (Jethro) of the Midianites, he left Sinai as a friend of God (Reuel).

When Jethro came to Sinai, he apparently also brought his son Hobab with him. When Jethro (or Reuel) left Sinai to return to his people (Ex 18:27), he also apparently left Hobab to stay with Moses and Zipporah. The inference here is that he would stay with them while they camped in Sinai. (Remember Sinai was part of the Midianites' territory.) Perhaps, he stayed to assist them while they encamped on his people's land. But now the Israelites are leaving Sinai, Hobab's assignment is concluded, and he is preparing to return to his home.

The name Hobab means "beloved". You may recall that our first encounter with Jethro's family is when Moses defends Jethro's seven daughters while they are watering their father's flock (Ex 2:16-17), a responsibility that Moses later assumes as Zipporah's husband. All of this tells me that Hobab was either very young when Moses first came on the scene or he was born to Jethro after Moses and Zipporah were married. Regardless, he was a son of Jethro's older age; he was the son whose arrival Jethro awaited for many years and he named him Hobab, his beloved son. The "beloved" son, perhaps the only son, of this "friend of God" (Reuel) dwelt among the people to help them, and perhaps to show them how to live in the wilderness of Sinai. This would have been a tremendous sacrifice for Jethro to leave Hobab there in the wilderness with the people. This sacrifice demonstrates Jethro's love for Moses and for the people of God.

But now it was time for Hobab to return to his father's house, to return to the father that he loved, and to return to the comforts and the favor of his father's house. But Moses pleads with him to stay with the Israelites. He says, "Hobab, you are a good shepherd. You know the places in the wilderness we should camp. You know where the green pastures are. You know the location of the quiet waters. Help guide us in the path that God leads us in. Dwell among us and share in all the good things God has promised to do for His people." We do not see Hobab say "no" a second time. It would appear that Hobab stayed with the Israelites and dwelt among them. In Judges 4:11 we see the descendants of Hobab inhabiting the Promised Land with the people.

As this people journeyed through the wilderness, God provided a beloved son, an only son, to shepherd them, to lead them beside green pastures and beside the still waters. He provided this son to help them journey through the wilderness, and to show them how. Though God was leading them, and though His presence dwelt in their midst, He had provided this one to live and walk among them.

. . .

Later God would send another son to dwell among this people – His beloved Son, His only Son. He would come as a Good Shepherd to teach His people, to lead His people and to show them how to live. The Father would deprive Himself of the companionship of the Son, and the Son would deprive Himself of the comfort of His home and the companionship of the Father.

Sometimes, even when we see God's activity all around us, and even when God's people surround us, we can feel alone as we journey through the wilderness. The Father sent His Son so that we might never be alone in the wilderness. Just like Hobab stayed with the children of Israel, this Beloved Son, Jesus, will never leave us or forsake us. Take heart, sojourner; the Beloved Son is traveling this wilderness path with you.

* * *

10

THE LESSONS OF TABERAH

The foreign rabble who were traveling with the Israelites began to crave the good things of Egypt, and the people of Israel also began to complain. "Oh, for some meat!" they exclaimed. "We remember all the fish we used to eat for free in Egypt. And we had all the cucumbers, melons, leeks, onions, and garlic that we wanted. But now our appetites are gone, and day after day we have nothing to eat but this manna!" The people soon began to complain to the LORD about their hardships; and when the LORD heard them, his anger blazed against them. Fire from the LORD raged among them and destroyed the outskirts of the camp. The people screamed to Moses for help; and when he prayed to the LORD, the fire stopped. After that, the area was known as Taberah--"the place of burning"--because fire from the LORD had burned among them there.

Numbers 11:4-6, 1-3

* * *

The order of these verses has intentionally been reversed so we can clearly see the cause and effect relationship of what is happening in this passage. The cause is the lusting and murmuring of the people; the effect is the judgment of God at Taberah. The murmuring started with the "foreign rabble". These were the people that were not a part of any specific tribe of Israel. More than likely, they were the offspring of marriages between children of Egypt and children of Israel. Having never felt like, nor been treated like, they were a part of Egypt; they joined with the children of Israel in the exodus from Egypt. But since the children of Israel had organized into clans, families and tribes as they were leaving the wilderness of Sinai, they no longer felt like they were a part of Israel.

They had no place under one of the banners of Israel. They were relegated to the outskirts of the camp, and there they began to crave the things of Egypt.

Their diet in Egypt was almost exclusively fish, particularly during the hot months of April and May; and now at that same time of year, they thought of the fresh fish they used to eat. (i wouldn't be surprised if they used to complain about always having to eat fish when they lived in Egypt!) They thought of the fish and the cucumbers and the melons and the leeks and the onions and the garlic and the.... - that they used to eat for free! Now somewhere i remember reading that these people were crying out for help because of their bondage while they were in Egypt, but what this group was remembering was the free food! Somehow they had forgotten their labor, their toil, their taskmasters and the sting of the whip on their backs. Somehow they had forgotten that nothing in Egypt was free; it came at great price!

It is amazing to reflect on all that the people had seen God accomplish on their behalf, from their deliverance from Egypt to date. And yet, this group was longing to be back in slavery. They had left their homes seeking the fortunes of the Promised Land, but their hearts were still in bondage. They sought after the trappings of their enslavement and ignored its cost and its consequence. Heed the lessons of Taberah; God will not stand by while we lust for the trappings of our life in sin.

And their contention began to infect others. That is the very same problem that Paul warned the church in Corinth about when he wrote, "*Do you not know that a little leaven leavens the whole lump? Therefore purge out the old leaven, that you may be a new lump, since you truly are unleavened. For indeed Christ, our Passover, was sacrificed for us*" (1 Cor 5:6-7 NKJ). Leaven is the heart that is in bondage to the sin and slavery of Egypt, that is seeking its own fulfillment in the Promised Land. It is the heart that seeks the trappings of sin and has grown cold to the fruit of faithfulness. It is a heart that has never truly been transformed, but goes through the motions of the pretense of transformation. And this group is not only a miserable group themselves; they desire to multiply their ranks and make everyone around them miserable as well.

There is only one cure for leaven in the lump. Paul wrote, "Purge out the old leaven." And that is what the LORD did at Taberah; He sent His purifying fire to purge out the leaven in order to purify the loaf. The rabble had not turned to Him, and now He would turn from them, purging them from among His people.

God still uses fire to purify His people today. He allows us to go through fire in our journey personally to remove the impurities, the leaven, and the sin in our lives so that we are not in bondage to sin and rendered ineffective for His purpose. And if we resist His transformation, He will at some point allow us to experience the purging fire of Taberah so that we do not leaven the loaf – His body, the church.

Heed the lessons of Taberah; do not resist His work. Do not resist His cleansing fire. Allow Him to remove the impurities and render you effective for His purpose. After all, that's why He led you on this journey through the wilderness to begin with.

* * *

11

THE LOAD IS FAR TOO HEAVY

Moses heard all the families standing in front of their tents weeping, and the LORD became extremely angry. Moses was also very aggravated. And Moses said to the LORD, "Why are you treating me, your servant, so miserably? What did I do to deserve the burden of a people like this? I can't carry all these people by myself! The load is far too heavy! I'd rather you killed me than treat me like this. Please spare me this misery!" Then the LORD said to Moses, "Summon before me seventy of the leaders of Israel. Bring them to the Tabernacle to stand there with you. I will come down and talk to you there. I will take some of the Spirit that is upon you, and I will put the Spirit upon them also. They will bear the burden of the people along with you, so you will not have to carry it alone.

Numbers 11:10-11, 14-17

* * *

As the people murmured, they dishonored God; and they directed it toward Moses. A wise man told me early in ministry, "If you're being led by the Lord, be mindful to pass all the praise on to Him, and all the criticism as well." A difficulty we sometimes have is that we want to hang on to some of it. We want to keep some of the praise; and as in this case, we tend to take the criticism and hold on to it personally as well. When we try to hold on to the praise, we will get too big for our britches; and when we try to hold on to the protest, we will end up having a "pity-party". When we try to hold on to either one, we will be adding more to our load than God intended; and the load will get heavier and heavier. At that point the ministry that God has called us to, and the service that He has placed us in, will cease to be a blessing and will become a burden – a "load that is far too heavy". When that happens, we will cry out to God to be taken out from under the burden; but the lesson we need to see today is that God never intended for us to be under the burden. Jesus said, *"My yoke fits perfectly, and the burden I give you is light*" (Matt 11:30).

You will know you are under a burden that God never intended when you overvalue your own performance in God's work. Moses said, "I can't carry all these people by myself!" As if he was carrying them at all! Who parted the Red Sea? Who defeated every enemy? Who provided for every need? We are very good at possessing ministry; we talk about his ministry or her ministry or my ministry. The truth of the matter is, it is God's ministry that He has chosen to accomplish through us. Don't ever get that confused and overvalue your part.

Secondly, Moses said to God, "I'd rather you killed me than treat me like this." Part of his overburdening came from when he undervalued the honor God had placed on him. Moses had been chosen by the Lord God Jehovah to be the instrument through which He led His people out of Egypt to the Promised Land. God didn't need to honor Moses, and Moses did not deserve to be honored. God <u>chose</u> to honor Moses. The same is true of us. God has given us rights and honor as His people (Rom 2:26), not because we are worthy but because He has chosen to do so. And what God has given value, no man can take away. With God's value comes the enablement and the empowerment to finish the task. Don't undervalue what God has valued – and don't allow others to do it either.

Next, Moses lost sight of the fact that this was God's assignment. God's assignment will always be far greater than anything we can do ourselves. God's work results in God's glory; if we could do it who would get the glory? We, like Moses, will find ourselves under a load that is far too heavy when we either overestimate our ability or underestimate God's ability. Take heart, there is nothing that He has placed before you that He does not have the strength to complete; and conversely, there is nothing that He has placed before you that you have the strength to complete apart from Him. So get out from under the load and give it to Him.

Lastly, watch for who God has surrounded you with to be co-laborers in His work. God has not called us to be "Lone Ranger" Christians. The seventy leaders that God told Moses to assemble were already in the camp. God had placed them there for just this purpose. Yes, Moses nominated the men, but it was God who qualified them. He had prepared them and He had gifted them. Now the Lord was preparing to fill them with His Spirit so that they would be fully equipped to accomplish His purpose.

As you journey down this wilderness path, are you under a load that is far too heavy? Get out from under it and give it to Him; He never intended for you to be under it – and He never will.

* * *

12

WHAT'S WRONG WITH WANTING MEAT?

Moses heard all the families standing in front of their tents weeping, and the LORD became extremely angry. Moses was also very aggravated. And Moses said to the LORD, "...Where am I supposed to get meat for all these people? They keep complaining and saying, 'Give us meat!' Then the LORD said to Moses, "... Tell the people to purify themselves, for tomorrow they will have meat to eat. Tell them, 'The LORD has heard your whining and complaints: "If only we had meat to eat! Surely we were better off in Egypt!" Now the LORD will give you meat, and you will have to eat it. ...You will eat it for a whole month until you gag and are sick of it. For you have rejected the LORD, who is here among you, and you have complained to him, "Why did we ever leave Egypt?" ' " Now the LORD sent a wind that brought quail from the sea and let them fall into the camp and all around it! For many miles in every direction from the camp there were quail flying about three feet above the ground. So the people went out and caught quail all that day and throughout the night and all the next day, too. No one gathered less than fifty bushels! They spread the quail out all over the camp. But while they were still eating the meat, the anger of the LORD blazed against the people, and he caused a severe plague to break out among them. So that place was called Kibroth-hattaavah--"the graves of craving"--because they buried the people there who had craved meat from Egypt.

Numbers 11:10-11, 13, 16, 18, 20, 31-34

* * *

It had been a year since God had provided the quail that night in the Wilderness of Sin (Ex 16). He had literally delivered it fresh to their doorstep; and nothing had ever tasted so good. Now the people craved meat again. But they didn't crave the meat of God; they craved the meat of Egypt. Their craving was so strong that they literally stood in front of their tents and wept. They wanted meat with their "whine"! And as their murmuring for the meat of Egypt increased, we read that the Lord became angry and Moses became aggravated.

Have you ever heard the expression, "Be careful what you pray for"? The people were crying out for the meat of Egypt, and God heard their cry and He answered them, "I will give you meat and you will have to eat it. You will eat it until you gag and are sick of it." By craving the meat of Egypt, they were rejecting God's provision; and by rejecting His provision, they were rejecting Him. So God was going to give them a thirty-day reminder of Egypt.

Imagine the excitement on the faces of the Israelites when that great sea of quail began to descend upon the camp. Imagine the multitude of birds. If we add up the bushels of quail gathered, allowing just the fifty-bushel minimum (though the average was probably more), that is THIRTY MILLION BUSHELS of quail. (i don't know how many quail there are in a bushel, i'll let you compute that – but it's a bunch of quail!) Immediately they stoked the cooking fires and prepared to dine on this feast of quail. But Scripture says that "while they were still eating" the LORD "caused a severe plague to break out among them." And those who had craved the meat from Egypt were buried in that place.

So what's wrong with wanting meat? Nothing is wrong with wanting meat, if it is the meat of the Lord. God tells us we are to ask Him, and He will withhold no good thing from us. They weren't asking for the meat of the Lord; they were murmuring for the meat of Egypt. And what did Egypt hold for the Israelites? It was a place of bondage and death; and the meat of Egypt brings with it that bondage and death. So the people truly received that for which they were murmuring. Did all of the people die? No, only those who craved the meat of Egypt. But there were others, probably many others, who experienced the sickness that the meat of Egypt can bring. They hadn't craved it, but they partook of it. And they called that place "the graves of craving" as a permanent reminder to the people.

So, what is the reminder to us? First, do not be blinded by the cravings for the meat of your Egypt – that place, that condition, that sin nature – which God has delivered you from. Allow what He has delivered you from to stay in Egypt. He defeated it there. It's buried there. If He has delivered you from that place, you are dead to it and you are to "reckon yourself dead" to that place (Rom 6:11). Don't hearken back for the dead things of Egypt, because that is all they will bring – sickness and death; rather seek those things that result in righteousness and sanctification (Rom 6:22). Our Lord had told us to want them, to seek them and to ask for them – and He will withhold no good thing (Psa 84:11).

Don't let this place in your journey be called the "graves of the craving" – a place of death; rather, seek the meat of the Lord and allow it to be a place of life – a permanent reminder of His faithfulness. Let this place be called the "cradle of His righteousness" (Matt 6:33).

* * *

13

ELDAD AND MEDAD

Two men, Eldad and Medad, were still in the camp when the Spirit rested upon them. They were listed among the leaders but had not gone out to the Tabernacle, so they prophesied there in the camp. A young man ran and reported to Moses, "Eldad and Medad are prophesying in the camp!" Joshua son of Nun, who had been Moses' personal assistant since his youth, protested, "Moses, my master, make them stop!" But Moses replied, "Are you jealous for my sake? I wish that all the LORD's people were prophets, and that the LORD would put his Spirit upon them all!"

Numbers 11:26-29

* * *

Eldad (meaning "God has loved") and Medad (meaning "beloved friend") were part of the group of seventy elders that God directed Moses to assemble. We don't know what tribe these men were a part of. We truly have no information about these men before or after this incident. For whatever reason these two men, who were probably brothers, had not gone to the Tabernacle with the rest of the elders; they were still in the camp. When the Holy Spirit came upon the elders, He came upon all of the elders, including these two who weren't in the tabernacle. We don't know why they weren't in the tabernacle, but there are lessons for us to learn as a result of their not being there. Oh, and isn't it interesting that theirs are the only names we know out of that group of seventy? Maybe the Lord does have a lesson for us to learn from these two men.

. . .

Well, anyway, they, like the others, began to prophesy; they began to speak the Truth of God, under the anointing of God, with the power of God. To this point, the people had only heard Moses and Aaron speak with that kind of authority. Thus the people in the camp marveled at the boldness and the authority with which these men spoke. One young man ran to tell Moses what was going on. Moses' protégé, Joshua, who himself was probably one of the seventy elders, demanded that Moses order them to stop. Joshua falsely assumed that only those gathered in the tabernacle were anointed to speak; only those under the purview of Moses were given that ability, and therefore allowing them to continue was an affront to Moses, the elders, and even the Lord. But Moses wisely saw that there was jealousy in Joshua's motivation, albeit perhaps a jealousy on behalf of Moses; and he wisely squelched that jealousy right there.

Moses knew what we too must realize: God does not operate under our limitations or our restrictions. **God's Spirit will fill whomever He chooses, wherever He chooses and whenever He chooses.** In those days, before the incarnation, crucifixion and resurrection of Christ, God's Spirit would fill those that He had anointed for a specific time and purpose. For example, these elders, many believe, were only able to speak with this kind of anointing for this one day. God's Spirit did not remain upon them continuously, as He did on Moses. Now, you and i, if we are followers of Jesus, have God's Spirit indwelling us; if we are saved we are indwelt – that is a condition that will not change from day to day. We are however to continuously seek the filling of His Spirit (Eph 5:18). And our Lord commands us to be cleansed vessels suitable for His filling and His use (2 Tim 2:21). We do not need to be in a specific place to be filled, but we must be in a specific posture – we must be postured as that cleansed vessel. Though Eldad and Medad were not in the Tabernacle, their absence was apparently not a result of any disobedience on their part, because God would not fill them with His Spirit if they were postured in disobedience. Moses wisely understood that God had chosen them right where they were for this time. God has led you to the place where you are right now for His purpose. The fact that He has led you is indicative that He has called you and chosen you; and He will fill you with His Spirit, if you will remain in a cleansed and usable posture.

Second, Moses' response to Joshua is also a lament. "I wish that all the LORD's people were prophets, and that the LORD would put his Spirit upon them all!" God desires to fill all of His people all of the time. He has saved us that we might be His instruments for the accomplishment of His purpose for eternity throughout this world at this time. It is not His intent or His plan that only some of us be filled with His Spirit; and it is not His plan that we only be filled with His Spirit some of the time. Why is it that 80% of the work is done by 20% of the church? Why is it that 80% of the financial resources given for the Lord's work are given by 20% of God's people? Why are we, like the Israelites, content to sit in our camps and complain, when our Lord desires us to be filled with His Spirit as champions of His Kingdom? The LORD desires to put His Spirit upon us all, all the time.

Third, Moses' response to Joshua is a testimony and a testament to the fact that there is to be no jealousy among God's people. God has chosen to accomplish His work through His people for His purpose and for His glory. We don't write the script, we don't direct the scene, and we don't control the outcome. The only jealousy that needs to exist within the body of Christ is an increased jealousy for the glory of God – a passion that no thing and no one act in any manner that would distract or detract from His glory.

Whether today you are gathered in the tabernacle or the camp of your wilderness journey, you are His tabernacle; you are His earthly dwelling place. Today He desires to fill you with His Spirit. Be like Eldad and Medad, no matter where you are, postured for His filling. And, oh yes, it will be conspicuous to those around you!

* * *

14

LITTLE SPARROW

In time, Reuel (Jethro) gave Moses one of his daughters, Zipporah, to be his wife. ...On the journey, when Moses and his family had stopped for the night, the LORD confronted Moses and was about to kill him. But Zipporah, his wife, took a flint knife and circumcised her son. She threw the foreskin at Moses' feet and said, "What a blood-smeared bridegroom you are to me!"...Some time before this, Moses had sent his wife, Zipporah, and his two sons to live with Jethro, his father-in-law. The name of Moses' first son was Gershom, for Moses had said when the boy was born, "I have been a stranger in a foreign land." The name of his second son was Eliezer, for Moses had said at his birth, "The God of my fathers was my helper; he delivered me from the sword of Pharaoh." Jethro now came to visit Moses, and he brought Moses' wife and two sons with him. They arrived while Moses and the people were camped near the mountain of God. ...While they were at Hazeroth, Miriam and Aaron criticized Moses because he had married a Cushite woman.

Exodus 2:21; 4:24-25; 18:2-5; Numbers 12:1

* * *

When Moses fled from Egypt, he settled in the land of Midian. God had prepared him through his time in Pharaoh's palace, and now He would prepare him through his time in Midian. God knew all that Moses would require to accomplish His work. He knew the preparation that was needed, and He knew the companions that would compliment him for the journey. God taught him how to tend sheep and God taught him how to be a husband and a father. To fulfill his assignment in leading the people of Israel, Moses would need to know how to be a shepherd, a husband and a father.

God gave Moses a companion, a helpmate – her name was Zipporah, meaning "little sparrow". She was the eldest daughter of the Midianite priest and prince – Jethro. Jethro gave Moses his firstborn daughter Zipporah because of the bravery, faithfulness and loyalty that Moses displayed in those early days in Midian.

The sparrow, though humble in stature, is a resilient little migratory bird. It is a species of bird that stays its course regardless of what it encounters. When Jesus referred to the birds of the air in His Sermon on the Mount, and the Father's care and concern for them, i picture the sparrow. And Jesus said the Father meets their every need – and they live out their lives with a confident resolve in their Creator's promise. It is that kind of faithful determination that we see expressed in Zipporah's life.

Zipporah was not a wallflower. She and her sisters bravely tended their father's flocks before Moses came on the scene. They would routinely have to contend and compete with the shepherds for watering rights for their flocks. Though they often were bested in their contention with the shepherds, they did not shrivel or shrink from their adversaries.

When Moses came home from his time at the burning bush, he announced to Jethro and Zipporah what God had told him to do. Zipporah packed up herself and their sons and made preparation to leave the only home she had ever known to follow her husband on his "mission from God". We do not read about the thoughts that went through Zipporah's mind. She was preparing to journey to Egypt as the wife of a fugitive of Pharaoh. She had no idea what fate awaited them in Egypt. She had heard no word from God – but her husband had. And she proceeded to walk with her husband in his obedience to his God.

Enroute, they arrived at an inn. God was prepared to put Moses to death for his disobedience in failing to circumcise his second son Eliezer. This is probably the result of Moses and Zipporah being unequally yoked. Moses had probably indulged Zipporah in his delay in circumcising Eliezer. She had endured his circumcision of their firstborn Gershom, but the practice probably seemed barbaric to her and lacking any conviction to obey God in this regard she convinced her husband to delay in his obedience. But on this day God would not be put off, and an angel of the Lord stood ready to slay Moses. God could not use Moses as His vessel of honor to bring about the deliverance of His people if Moses continued in this state of disobedience to God. The boy must be circumcised now; and Moses, standing at the precipice of death is unable to do so. Zipporah, putting her fear aside, steps forward with knife in hand and circumcises their son. And as i said, i don't believe Zipporah was a wallflower, so i don't believe she made any attempt to hide her dislike and disdain for the practice, but she did what needed to be done to save her husband.

After that incident Moses sent her and their sons back to Jethro's house and continued without them to Egypt. There they remained until Jethro reunited them with Moses in the Wilderness of Sinai. From there on, they journeyed together as a family, with the children of Israel through the wilderness. No further mention is made of Zipporah after they are reunited at Sinai, with the exception of this reference to her of disdain by Miriam and Aaron. And i can't help but wonder if the motivation for this criticism from Miriam is jealousy over Zipporah's position of respect and influence as Moses' wife. As for Aaron, he continues to demonstrate an inability to say no when appropriate, so when Miriam begins to criticize Zipporah he again takes the spineless approach and goes along with Miriam. You see, i believe Zipporah came to see this God of Moses as the Lord God Jehovah – the One True God. i believe that she, just like her father, Jethro, and her brother, Hobab, came to follow the One True God. And as a result, this helpmate and companion of Moses – this little sparrow – with faithful determination became an even greater companion and helpmate to Moses as he led the people and an encouragement to those around her.

As you journey in the wilderness, be that helpmate that God intends – that little sparrow – faithfully determined and confident in your Creator.

* * *

15

DON'T MESS WITH GOD'S ANOINTED

While they were at Hazeroth, Miriam and Aaron criticized Moses because he had married a Cushite woman. They said, "Has the LORD spoken only through Moses? Hasn't he spoken through us, too?" But the LORD heard them… Then the LORD descended in the pillar of cloud and stood at the entrance of the Tabernacle. "Aaron and Miriam!" he called, and they stepped forward. And the LORD said to them, "Now listen to me! Even with prophets, I the LORD communicate by visions and dreams. But that is not how I communicate with my servant Moses. He is entrusted with my entire house. I speak to him face to face, directly and not in riddles! He sees the LORD as he is. Should you not be afraid to criticize him?" The LORD was furious with them, and he departed. As the cloud moved from above the Tabernacle, Miriam suddenly became white as snow with leprosy... So Moses cried out to the LORD, "Heal her, O God, I beg you!" And the LORD said to Moses, "If her father had spit in her face, wouldn't she have been defiled for seven days? Banish her from the camp for seven days, and after that she may return." So Miriam was excluded from the camp for seven days, and the people waited until she was brought back before they traveled again.
Numbers 12:1-2, 5-10, 13-15

* * *

Hazeroth was an encampment in the wilderness of Paran. Hazeroth was characterized by, and in fact is the Hebrew name for, enclosures of stone "in which thick bundles of thorny acacia are inserted, the tangled branches and long needle-like spikes forming a perfectly impenetrable hedge around the tents and cattle which they sheltered" (Easton's Bible Dictionary). Just as the thorny needles of the acacia could physically cut and sting anyone or anything attempting to cross those enclosures, so can thorny words and mean-spirited criticisms cut and sting their intended victim.

In this place of needles and stings, Miriam (Moses' sister) and Aaron cast their verbal barbs at Moses. As we have already seen, this criticism originated with Miriam, and Aaron foolishly went along. Remember that this event followed the selection of the seventy elders. The criticisms that Miriam leveled seem to relate to that selection process. First, Miriam complains about Zipporah, apparently having to do with her influence on Moses in his selection process. Second, she complains that Moses selected the seventy elders unilaterally without consulting she and Aaron. All in all, her complaints stem from a personal resentment that she wasn't included in the process; thus she decides to vent her hurt and anger that stem from a selfish ambition by leveling these criticisms at Moses. And apparently they didn't approach their brother privately with these concerns but openly criticized him before the people. There was one other Person listening that they had lost sight of, and He wasn't going to sit by idly while they leveled their criticisms at His anointed.

As God's anointed, He had called Moses. He had entrusted Moses with a people to lead, a position and a responsibility to heed, and a path that he must follow. He enabled Moses to hear His voice, to speak with Him and to see His face. That calling and that anointing did not come without accountability, but that accountability was to God. It was an accountability that no one else there had, and as we see later, it was an accountability that would keep Moses from entering into the Promised Land. But on this day God wanted Miriam, Aaron and all the people to know that if you "mess" with His anointed, you "mess" with the Lord God Jehovah. Moses in his humility may have overlooked the criticism, but God Almighty would not. Moses in his compassion may intercede on his sister's behalf, but God Almighty would not immediately remove the consequence for her sin. God kept all the people in that place of needles and stings, and permitted Miriam to suffer from leprosy for seven days so that she and all of the Israelites would know that God does not take criticism of His servant's lightly.

God chose to afflict Miriam with leprosy. As we look at how seriously God takes the criticism of His servants, we must see the correlation between Miriam's actions and the effects of the disease with which she was afflicted. The disfigurement and the disablement of the disease causes those who are afflicted with it to be rejected and excluded from society. Miriam's selfish ambition for greater inclusion in Moses' leadership decisions in fact resulted in her exclusion from the people. Her outburst of critical rejection of Moses in fact resulted in her rejection from all the people. And the people would not move from this spot until this lesson had been brought home. Thus they waited there for seven days.

God would have us heed this lesson on our wilderness journey as well. We are not to criticize those that God has placed in authority over us; we are to encourage them and we are to afford them the honor that is due them. When disagreements or misunderstandings arise, we are to approach him/her with all of the respect that he/she is due as God's anointed. Even David, before he was crowned king, but after he had been anointed by Samuel, being pursued by a King Saul who was no longer seeking God, said that he could not raise his hand in any way against the Lord's anointed (1 Sam 26:23). But you ask, "What if the leader is being disobedient to God and His Word?" Then we should follow the steps that our Lord has given us in Matthew 18. But that is a subject for another time. Remember, this is God's anointed; if discipline is needed, God will make sure that it is administered. In the meantime, remember the lesson of Hazeroth and don't "mess" with God's anointed.

* * *

16

COMMISSIONED AND SENT

The LORD now said to Moses, "Send men to explore the land of Canaan, the land I am giving to Israel. Send one leader from each of the twelve ancestral tribes." So Moses did as the LORD commanded him. He sent out twelve men, all tribal leaders of Israel, from their camp in the wilderness of Paran.
Numbers 13:1-3

* * *

During my years as an associate pastor, i have been blessed to serve with some tremendous servants of God on various committees. i have seen how God has uniquely prepared these men and women for their respective assignments and called them into their positions on these committees for just such a time. i have seen the strength that has come from the complimenting strength and giftedness of each member, as each one was representative of the diversity of the Body. There is strength in that diversity; and there is a confidence that comes from seeing God take that diversity and create unanimity under His leadership.

This was just such a group of men. They were leaders of their respective tribes. These were men that were respected and trusted by their peers. Allow me to introduce you to this who's-who of Israelite society.

At the top of the list is Shammua, son of Zaccur, representing the tribe of

Reuben. His name indicates that his achievements and his distinguishing qualities were celebrated, not only throughout the tribe of Reuben, but among all of the Israelites. Among this tribe of over two million people, Shammua was admired, respected and renowned.

Shaphat, son of Hori, represented the tribe of Simeon. In every area of service and fraternity, the tribes of Reuben and Simeon worked, camped and traveled together. Shaphat's name implies that he was recognized among the tribes as being sound in his judgment and fair in his deliberations. He was respected for his wisdom and his discernment.

The tribe of Judah, the leader of the twelve tribes as they journeyed, was represented by Caleb, son of Jephunneh. Caleb was known for his courage, his faithfulness and his confidence in God. He was a man's man who had the ability to look at his circumstances in light of God's promises instead of the other way around.

Igal, son of Joseph, represented the tribe of Issachar. This tribe had the uncanny ability to be politically correct before it was in vogue and more often than not made savvy political alliances. Igal's name implies he had been redeemed from his enslavement prior to the exodus from Egypt. Either through political connections or wealth, Igal had not lived the life of a slave in Egypt, but at the same time he was not distrusted for this distinction but was respected by the other members of his tribe.

Hoshea, son of Nun, whom Moses renamed Joshua, represented the tribe of Ephraim. Hoshea means "salvation"; Joshua means "the Lord is salvation". Joshua's name change reflects a life that was surrendered and submitted to God. As we have already seen, Joshua had a heart to seek God and a faith in His Person, His power and His purpose.

The tribe of Benjamin was represented by Palti, son of Raphu. Palti's name reflects that he was a man that was fearless; a man that walked with boldness and confidence. The men of his tribe respected Palti; but some of them would also admit that they lived in fear of him.

Gaddiel, son of Sodi, represented the tribe of Zebulun. God had conspicuously blessed Gaddiel, perhaps in wealth and possessions, or perhaps in business acumen; Gaddiel had the ability to take a lemon of a situation and turn it into lemonade.

Gaddi, son of Susi, wasn't as blessed as Gaddiel, but he was considered to be a fortunate man. Representing the tribe of Manasseh, Gaddi had also experienced the blessings of God in a conspicuous fashion that brought him to the forefront of leadership among the people of this tribe.

The tribe of Dan was represented by Ammiel, son of Gemalli. This son of the Danites was also a son of wealth and of influence, and perhaps one of the more ostentatious and pretentious in his bearing.

Sethur, son of Michael, and Nahbi, son of Vophsi, representing the tribes of Asher and Naphtali, respectively, were apparently both the strong, silent type. They were just the opposite of Ammiel; they commanded the respect of their tribes through their lack of pretense and through their carriage of humility.

Lastly, the tribe of Gad was represented by Geuel, son of Maki. The tribe of Gad walked in the shadow of the Reubenites and the Simeonites, and Geuel walked in the shadow of Shammua and Shaphat. His name however means "the majesty of God" and his life reflected the blessings of the majestic hand of God. He would not step forward as a leader of the twelve, but they would not intimidate him either.

There is the commission of explorers – quite an impressive group. As you can see, they are a diverse group. Each one has strengths, and each one has weaknesses. But their makeup will compliment one another. And they are being sent on a mission of missions to explore the land of milk and honey that God is giving to them. They will be the first to see the fruit of the promises of God. What everyone, up to this point, has visualized by faith, they will now see by sight. Imagine the honor to be chosen. Imagine the privilege to go and see. Imagine the responsibility to be commissioned and sent. As they go they must pray that they not be detracted by their own abilities or their own wisdom; they are on God's mission, not their own. When you have the talent that this group has, it is easy to lean on your own understanding.

. . .

You, too, have been commissioned and sent, heed this counsel: *"Trust in the LORD with all your heart; do not depend on your own understanding. Seek His will in all you do, and He will direct your paths"* (Prov 3:5-6).

* * *

17

MAKE SURE YOU UNDERSTAND YOUR MISSION

Moses gave the men these instructions as he sent them out to explore the land: "Go northward through the Negev into the hill country. See what the land is like and find out whether the people living there are strong or weak, few or many. What kind of land do they live in? Is it good or bad? Do their towns have walls or are they unprotected? How is the soil? Is it fertile or poor? Are there many trees? Enter the land boldly, and bring back samples of the crops you see." (It happened to be the season for harvesting the first ripe grapes.)
Numbers 13:17-20

* * *

We've already looked at the make-up of the contingent that was being sent ahead to explore the Promised Land. They were leaders, selected for their wisdom, trustworthiness and insight. They were handpicked to match their assignment. You wouldn't have found twelve sharper people to send on this mission.

Moses demonstrated capable leadership in clearly defining the questions they were being sent to answer. As i have already mentioned, i have had the blessing of working with a number of church committees. In that process, a critical starting point for every new committee or any new member on an existing committee, is to make sure there is a clear definition of the committee's purpose, and a clear understanding on everyone's part of that purpose. What is the responsibility that they are being charged with? What are the boundaries of their purview? What authority does the committee have? Who does the committee report to and to whom is the committee accountable? Is there a clear and concise written statement of purpose that answers each of these questions? Without this information clearly defined, a committee can flounder and not know how or where to begin, or it can begin to become sidetracked, moving in directions other than those for which it was formed. The leader and the committee must continually evaluate their activity and progress against their purpose to insure that they are staying on task and not drifting.

Moses specifically told the men where they were to explore. They were being sent northward out of the Wilderness of Paran through the hills to southern Canaan. They were being sent to explore the closest entry point into the Promised Land. Up until now, God had led the people on a circuitous route out of Egypt. He had done so to bypass the land of the Philistines (Ex 13:17), to deliver His people through the Red Sea to the glory of His Name (Ex 13:18 and Josh 2:10), and to bring them though Mount Sinai so that they might worship Him in that place according to His promise (Ex 3:12). But now He was ready to lead His children directly into the Promised Land. It was to that entry place that these men were being sent.

Moses specifically told the men what they were to explore. They were to explore and report on the inhabitants and their encampments, and the land and its crop production. How many people live there? What are their demographics? Do they live in fortified cities or unprotected encampments? Is the land fertile or fruitless? What can we anticipate as we enter into the land? What kind of life and livelihood will the land provide? Bring us back samples so that we can see for ourselves what a "land flowing with milk and honey" produces! Go quickly; explore the land and bring us your report.

Today this group would be called a reconnaissance team. They were sent to reconnoiter the land – to survey it, in preparation for inhabiting it. They were to explore and examine the land and report their findings to Moses and the elders. This group was never sent to evaluate the feasibility of inhabiting the land. That was never the question. God had said, "I will bring you in to the land; and I will completely destroy your enemies." Their mission was not to evaluate how; their mission was solely to explore where and what. They didn't even have to research when; God's time was now. So did they misunderstand the question, or did they allow themselves to be distracted by the circumstances from what they were authorized and commissioned to explore? Their concern was never to be the "how"; God was always in charge of that.

The same is true of us. Our Lord has given us our charge. He has defined our purpose and given us our commission. In that commission, He has defined what and where; and He has clearly shown us that the when is now. And He has told us to follow Him and He will direct the how. And what is our commission? "When the Holy Spirit has come upon you" (when) "go and make disciples" (what) "of all nations" (where) "and be sure of this: I am with you always" (how). That is our purpose; that is our charge. Just like those twelve men, God has called us, chosen us, gifted us and equipped us for our charge. He will go before us. Let us not be distracted by the circumstances we encounter on our wilderness journey. Make sure you understand your mission; and then, let's stick to it!

* * *

18

THE MAJORITY REPORT

So they went up and explored the land.... When they came to what is now known as the valley of Eshcol, they cut down a cluster of grapes so large that it took two of them to carry it on a pole between them! ...After exploring the land for forty days, the men returned to Moses, Aaron, and the people of Israel at Kadesh in the wilderness of Paran. They reported to the whole community what they had seen and showed them the fruit they had taken from the land. This was their report to Moses: "We arrived in the land you sent us to see, and it is indeed a magnificent country--a land flowing with milk and honey. Here is some of its fruit as proof. But the people living there are powerful, and their cities and towns are fortified and very large.... We can't go up against them! They are stronger than we are!" So they spread discouraging reports about the land among the Israelites: "The land we explored will swallow up any who go to live there. All the people we saw were huge. We even saw giants there, the descendants of Anak. We felt like grasshoppers next to them, and that's what we looked like to them!" ...Then the ten scouts who had incited the rebellion against the LORD by spreading discouraging reports about the land were struck dead with a plague before the LORD.

Numbers 13:21, 23, 25-28, 31-33; 14:36-37

* * *

As Americans, we live in a democracy, and a fundamental rule of a democracy is that the majority rules. But as God's people, we live in a theocracy, and a fundamental rule of a theocracy is that God rules, regardless of what the majority says. He cannot be outvoted. Remember this equation: "GOD > Majority". God is always greater than the majority

– and He always will be. Once you have heard from God, you have heard the majority report; no other report is relevant. There is no counsel that will stand against that of the LORD; there is no other opinion that matters. You don't have to take the matter to a vote. The well-known axiom, "God said it, so that settles it" applies. Too many times God's people have gotten turned "cattywampus" by following a majority opinion that had nothing to do with God's direction. Let us look at the lesson God would teach us through the circumstances of this majority report.

We've already looked at the makeup of this group (capable and skilled), as well as their mission (clear and defined). Now after forty days of surveying the land, they return to give their report to Moses and the people. The report starts out strong: "It is indeed a magnificent country, a land flowing with milk and honey." It is everything that God has promised that it will be. Its fruit is better than anything they have ever seen and greater than they have ever imagined. Look at the size of these grapes! Then their report took a turn for the worse with the introduction of the word "but". "The people there are powerful, their cities are fortified, and we can't go up against them!" The vote of the committee was 10 to 2. That is an 83% majority. In politics today, that would be considered to be a landslide vote. The argument was compelling: "The people are stronger than we are. We are like grasshoppers compared to them. If we go there, the land will swallow us up. It would be better for us if we went back to Egypt." And this report was coming from men like Shammua and Shaphat. These were well-respected men. If they didn't think the land should be entered, then who could disagree with them? If ten out of twelve of the men say that we shouldn't enter the Promised Land, surely that is the right decision. God gave these men wisdom and the ability to think, didn't He? i mean, walking by faith doesn't mean that we disengage our brains, does it? God must not have clearly seen the circumstances that awaited the people in the Promised Land; or perhaps, Moses misunderstood what God had said. So the people heard the majority report; they accepted it and they turned their backs on God.

This same scenario occurs in our homes and our churches today. What are we to do when the majority report does not line up with what we believe God has told us to do? First, go back and look at what God has told you. God had repeatedly told the Israelites that He was bringing them into the land and that He would defeat their enemies. He told them before they left Egypt (Ex 3:8), He told them as they were leaving Egypt (Ex 13:5), He told them at Sinai before they formed the golden calf (Ex 23:23, 28), and He told them again at Sinai after the golden calf had been destroyed (Ex

33:2 and Ex 34:11). God left no margin for doubt about His intentions. He clearly gave the people a promise. In our case, we must go back and look at the promise God has given us. He is not "hoping we figure it out"; God will make His promise very clear to us.

Second, look at the circumstances that have been encountered in light of God's promise. Now, don't ever get that backwards! That is the mistake that the majority made that day, and unfortunately, that the majority of us make today. It's easy for us to look at the majority here and shake our heads at their faithlessness, but we do the same thing. Too often we look at God's promise in light of our circumstances, we start to get overwhelmed and discouraged and we begin to distrust God. Remember that your God is bigger than ANY circumstance you will encounter. *"By His mighty power… He is able to accomplish infinitely more than we would ever dare to ask or hope"* (Eph 3:20). Look at those circumstances through God's promise; He will use the circumstances ahead to fulfill His purpose while He fulfills His promise.

Third, don't think that you have to figure it all out. If, from where you're standing, you can't see how God is going to work all of this out – that's okay, He's God and you're not! That's why He has commanded us to walk by faith, and not by sight. Trust Him to accomplish His work His way. Those ten very talented men tried to figure it out and they couldn't. So instead of provoking the people to faith they incited them to discouragement. Instead of walking in God's victory into the Promised Land, they were buried due to their faithlessness in the wilderness.

Remember God, all by Himself, is the majority. He is the Beginning, the End, the Author and the Finisher. Heed His report and no other. His land of promise lies ahead. He's led you this far; trust Him to lead you <u>all</u> of the way!

* * *

19

THE MINORITY REPORT

After exploring the land for forty days, the men returned to Moses, Aaron, and the people of Israel at Kadesh in the wilderness of Paran. They reported to the whole community what they had seen and showed them the fruit they had taken from the land. ...Two of the men who had explored the land, Joshua son of Nun and Caleb son of Jephunneh, ...said to the community of Israel, "The land we explored is a wonderful land! And if the LORD is pleased with us, he will bring us safely into that land and give it to us. It is a rich land flowing with milk and honey, and he will give it to us! Do not rebel against the LORD, and don't be afraid of the people of the land. They are only helpless prey to us! They have no protection, but the LORD is with us! Don't be afraid of them!" But the whole community began to talk about stoning Joshua and Caleb. ...Then the LORD said, "...Because you complained against me, none of you who are twenty years old or older and were counted in the census will enter the land I swore to give you. The only exceptions will be Caleb son of Jephunneh and Joshua son of Nun. ...Of the twelve who had explored the land, only Joshua and Caleb remained alive.

Numbers 13:25, 26; 14:6-10, 20, 29, 38

* * *

Joshua and Caleb saw the exact same things that the other ten men saw. They all had seen the richness of the land. They saw the size of the people and the strength of their fortifications. But what the majority saw as giants, the minority saw as prey; and what the majority saw as obstacles that could not be overcome, the minority saw as opportunities for God to demonstrate His power. The majority saw their defenses; the minority saw their vulnerability. So what caused the majority and the minority to see different things when they were looking at the exact same things? It was the eyes through which they were looking. The majority looked through the eyes of fear, and the minority through the eyes of faith.

Eyes of fear will always look up at the obstacles from man's perspective; eyes of faith will always look down at the obstacles from God's perspective. Eyes of fear will always gaze out from under the circumstances; eyes of faith will always look over the circumstances in light of God's promises. Eyes of fear will always be blinded by the visible; eyes of faith will always be illuminated by the unseen assurance of God.

The report of faith will all too often be the minority report. Our propensity, a characteristic of our flesh nature, will always be to look ahead through eyes of fear. We pride ourselves on our seasoned objectivity, our pragmatism and our "feet-firmly-planted-on-the-ground" common sense, when in fact, what we need is an uncommon sense that comes from ears attuned to God's voice, hearts and hands willing to do His bidding, and feet willing to follow Him wherever He leads. Let's face it, was it common sense that led Noah to invest 100 years in the construction of a big boat in the middle of dry land in preparation for a flood in a place that had never seen rain? Was it pragmatism that prompted Abraham to pack up his family and his possessions and leave their home in Haran when he had absolutely no idea where he was going? Was it seasoned objectivity that prompted Peter, Andrew, James and John to leave their successful fishing businesses to follow the penniless son of a carpenter? In each instance there would have been a majority report that said these men were crazy. i can hear it now, "Peter, it's one thing to have your head in the clouds, but plant your feet on the ground, man, you have a family to think about." Or how about another familiar moment in history – the Israelite army is trembling before a giant that is too big to fight, when up steps a shepherd boy who sees the giant as too big to miss? God's call on our lives to step out by faith will be a call to step out of the majority into the minority. It is a call from the mainstream to the "faith-stream".

Caleb and Joshua were severely criticized by the majority for the position they took. As a matter of fact, the community began to talk about stoning them. But these men never once backed away from their stand of faith. They never once compromised their conviction. And they never once doubted the promise of God.

• • •

As a result of their faithfulness, and as a result of their courageous obedience, those two men were the only two out of over 600,000 men to survive the forty-year wandering and enter the Promised Land. The critics of the minority report all perished in the wilderness; only these two experienced the blessings of the land of milk and honey. The writer of Hebrews writes, *"So, you see, it is impossible to please God without faith. Anyone who wants to come to Him must believe that there is a God and that He rewards those who sincerely seek Him"* (Heb 11:6). God was displeased with the majority report, but He rewarded these two. God is a Rewarder of those who walk by faith.

So as you explore what lies ahead, are the obstacles too great for God to overcome? Does the land seem too far off for God to be able to get you there? Does the journey seem too difficult for God to enable you to endure? Does none of it make any sense apart from the promise that you know God has given you? Don't use your common sense; use the uncommon sense God has given you. Stick with the minority report and look at the land ahead in light of God's promise. God will reward your faithfulness.

* * *

20

TURNED BACK TO THE WILDERNESS

Then all the people began weeping aloud, and they cried all night. Their voices rose in a great chorus of complaint against Moses and Aaron. "We wish we had died in Egypt, or even here in the wilderness!" they wailed. "Why is the LORD taking us to this country only to have us die in battle? Our wives and little ones will be carried off as slaves! Let's get out of here and return to Egypt!" And the LORD said to Moses, "How long will these people reject me? Will they never believe me, even after all the miraculous signs I have done among them? But as surely as I live, and as surely as the earth is filled with the LORD's glory, not one of these people will ever enter that land. They have seen my glorious presence and the miraculous signs I performed both in Egypt and in the wilderness, but again and again they tested me by refusing to listen. They will never even see the land I swore to give their ancestors. None of those who have treated me with contempt will enter it. Now turn around and don't go on toward the land where the Amalekites and Canaanites live. Tomorrow you must set out for the wilderness in the direction of the Red Sea."

Numbers 14:1-3, 11, 21-23, 25

* * *

These were God's people. These were the people that He had delivered from the bondage of Egypt so that through them He might reveal His Name and His glory to the nations. These were the people with whom God had made the covenant: *"If you will obey me and keep my covenant, you will be my own special treasure from among all the nations of the earth; for all the earth belongs to me. And you will be to me a kingdom of priests, my holy nation"* (Ex 19:5-6). And yet time and again since they had left

Egypt, the people had forgotten God's promise, doubted God's promise or rejected God's promise. Here they were right on the edge of receiving the land that God had promised them. They had heard the report that the land was truly a land flowing with milk and honey. It was all that God had promised it would be. God had led them here. He had defeated their enemies along the way. He had provided for their every need. He had repeated His promise, revealed His presence and redeemed His people. And now on the eve of what could have been the greatest day of their lives, and their history as a nation, the day they were to enter God's Promised Land, they chose to reject God and refused to enter into His Promised Land. By rejecting God in unbelief they were turning their backs on God. They were positioning their faces away from Him. It wasn't God who turned them back to the wilderness, it was they themselves – it was their unbelief. Those that despise the promise of God will be kept from it. However, God in His faithfulness would preserve His promise for their children.

God had set their faces toward the Promised Land. To this point every step in the wilderness had been leading them closer to this place and this day. Each step prepared them further for what was ahead. But now, as they turned their backs on God, their faces were set back toward the wilderness. The wilderness, instead of being a place of preparation would now be a place of judgment. Their sentence would come from their very own words. Since the people had placed their trust in the testimony of men (the majority report), they would now be destined to wander in the wilderness for forty years (one year for each day the men had explored the land). Instead of inheriting the Promised Land, this entire generation, save only Joshua and Caleb, would be buried in the wilderness.

Lest we jump to the conclusion that God uses the wilderness as a punishment, let's revisit its purpose. The fact is God uses the wilderness to humble us, to prove us and to show us what is in our hearts. It is a time of preparation and refinement. He also uses it to display His provision and His power working in and through our lives throughout the journey. God uses that time in the wilderness to give us a greater hunger and thirst for Him and for His desires. And in His perfect timing He will bring us out of the wilderness into His promised land. We will step from the trials of the wilderness into the rest and reward of His promise. It is hard to fathom that at this point the Israelites were hankering for the slavery of Egypt or the trials of the wilderness over the fruit of God's promised land. But instead of stepping forward by faith, they turned back out of fear and rejected God. The wilderness that now lay ahead would be a place of death and desolation for the generation that had withdrawn in unbelief.

How often have we chosen to turn our backs toward God and our faces towards the wilderness? How often have we in fear rejected God's promises and His Person, choosing to live out our lives in restless wanderings through the wilderness? We've rejected the unknown (the promised blessings of God) and turned to the known (the trials and difficulties of the wilderness) because we doubt God's promise. When all the time He is right there waiting for us to enter into His promise. But there will come the point that our rejection of God, our turning our back on Him, will prompt Him to turn us back to the wilderness. His promise having been rejected will now be beyond our grasp and we will be destined to live out the remainder of our lives in the wilderness.

Fellow sojourners, heed this lesson in the wilderness. Keep your face turned toward the God who has led you to this place; the same God who has led you this far, will lead you all of the way.

* * *

21

TOO LITTLE TOO LATE

Then the LORD said, "...Now turn around and don't go on toward the land where the Amalekites and Canaanites live. Tomorrow you must set out for the wilderness in the direction of the Red Sea." ...When Moses reported the LORD's words to the Israelites, there was much sorrow among the people. So they got up early the next morning and set out for the hill country of Canaan. "Let's go," they said. "We realize that we have sinned, but now we are ready to enter the land the LORD has promised us." But Moses said, "Why are you now disobeying the LORD's orders to return to the wilderness? It won't work. Do not go into the land now. You will only be crushed by your enemies because the LORD is not with you. When you face the Amalekites and Canaanites in battle, you will be slaughtered. The LORD will abandon you because you have abandoned the LORD." But the people pushed ahead toward the hill country of Canaan, despite the fact that neither Moses nor the Ark of the LORD's covenant left the camp. Then the Amalekites and the Canaanites who lived in those hills came down and attacked them and chased them as far as Hormah.

Numbers 14:20, 25, 39-45

* * *

"We know we sinned and we feel really bad about it. We are ready to obey God now and receive His promise." There was only one problem with this confession from the people – it was too little too late.

They did feel bad. They knew that they had fouled up big time! They knew that their complaints against God had just cost them an inheritance in the Promised Land, and that in exchange they had just settled for a burial plot in the wilderness. The reality of the consequence of their actions had begun to sink in. So now they were really sorry and ready to move forward as if they hadn't rebelled. "Lord, let's just go ahead as if it never happened. Forgive and forget! Let's move forward with Your plan. After all it's Your plan; You promised us. Just forgive us and let's move forward."

What we're hearing in the cries of the Israelites is remorse, not repentance. Remorse says, "i'm sorry for what i did because i am now hurting really bad." The focus of remorse is always on me and my consequence. Repentance says, "God, i have sinned against You. i have dishonored and hurt You." The focus of repentance is always on God and my rejection of Him. Remorse is always looking for the quickest way for me to get out from under the pain of the consequence and the most painless way for me to get back to the place that my needs are being met. Repentance is looking for the adjustment God would have me make to become rightly related to Him, no matter how difficult or painful that adjustment may be. Remorse is looking for the shortcut; repentance is looking for God's road of redemption. Remorse is looking for the whole incident to be put behind us; repentance understands that though forgiveness is immediate, restoration is a process. i can be remorseful without ever experiencing a change of heart; repentance, however, will begin with a broken and a contrite heart.

The next action that the Israelites took clearly revealed their unrepentant heart; their solution to sinning against God was to sin against God again. Instead of returning to the wilderness as God had commanded, they attempted to enter the Promised Land on their own accord. When we sin against God, we do not get to choose our path back to Him. He made the Way through His Son. We can only come to Him through His Way and we can only come to right relationship with Him through His Way. Our only choice is to go God's Way! A delay in our obedience is disobedience and God does not allow those opportunities to perch. Though God will always accomplish His purpose, and nothing we ever do will frustrate Him in that end, our delays, in the very least, will cause us to miss out on the fullness of the blessing we would have experienced if we had not delayed.

So the people pushed ahead without God going before them, and the Amalekites and the Canaanites overwhelmingly defeated them. In fact, the Amalekites and the Canaanites chased the Israelites all the way to

Hormah, which means, "complete destruction". That is a great reminder to us that when we push ahead out of remorse and try to manipulate God into negating that which our disobedience has cost us, we, too, will end up in Hormah; we, too, will experience defeat and destruction.

So what do i do if i have been disobedient to God? Is everything lost? Can i never come back into right relationship with Him again? By His grace that is not the case. He has promised us that "*if we confess our sins to him, he is faithful and just to forgive us and to cleanse us from every wrong*" (1 John 1:9). If we will turn to Him in repentance, He will place our feet on His path leading to our being rightly related to Him. It will be His path and He will be leading; and we will again experience His victory. Don't settle for less; and don't delay in responding to Him. Otherwise you, too, could end up in Hormah having given too little too late.

* * *

22

UNHOLY AMBITION

One day Korah son of Izhar, a descendant of Kohath son of Levi, conspired with Dathan and Abiram, the sons of Eliab, and On son of Peleth, from the tribe of Reuben. They incited a rebellion against Moses, involving 250 other prominent leaders, all members of the assembly. They went to Moses and Aaron and said, "You have gone too far! Everyone in Israel has been set apart by the LORD, and he is with all of us. What right do you have to act as though you are greater than anyone else among all these people of the LORD?" When Moses heard what they were saying, he threw himself down with his face to the ground. ...And the LORD said to Moses, "Then tell all the people to get away from the tents of Korah, Dathan, and Abiram." ...So all the people stood back from the tents of Korah, Dathan, and Abiram.... The earth opened up and swallowed the men, along with their households and the followers who were standing with them, and everything they owned. So they went down alive into the grave, along with their belongings. The earth closed over them, and they all vanished. All of the people of Israel fled as they heard their screams, fearing that the earth would swallow them, too.

Numbers 16:1-4, 23-24, 27, 32-34

* * *

We read in Scripture that *"all have sinned; all fall short of God's glorious standard"* (Rom 6:23). Sin, disobedience and rebellion are not limited to any one socio-economic stratum. You may recall that the last revolt that broke out in the camp was led by the "foreign rabble"; this time sons of distinction stepped forward to rebel against God and His plan. The ringleader was Korah, a Levite. Korah was the cousin of Moses and

Aaron. Korah's father, Izhar, was the brother of Amram, the father of Moses and Aaron. The tribe of Levi was subdivided into three family groups – the Gershonites, the Kohathites and the Merari. Moses, Aaron and Korah were all descendants of Kohath. The Kohathites were given the duty of caring for and transporting the Ark of the Covenant as well as the furnishings and utensils of the tabernacle. The ark represented God's presence wherever the people went, and as a Kohathite, Korah was charged with bearing the ark. But Korah had a greater ambition than to be the bearer of the Lord's covenant. He determined that he and his sons had as much of a birthright to the priesthood as Aaron and his sons. Korah also could have resented the fact that his cousin Elzaphan had been chosen by Moses to be the leader of the Kohathite families. For whatever reason, Korah was no longer content to serve as a "minister of the ark"; he demanded that he was entitled to a position of greater authority. His accusation was "What right do you have to act as though you are greater than anyone else?" What he was really saying was "What right do you have to act as though you are greater than me?" Do not be confused, Korah was not seeking position for others; he was seeking out his own interest to satisfy his own unholy ambition.

Korah enlisted Dathan and Abiram, the sons of Eliab, from the tribe of Reuben. He decided to lend credence to his complaint by enlisting others to join with him. Perhaps Dathan and Abiram were upset that the tribe of Judah had been given the place of honor in the camp, which they felt as the firstborn of Jacob, belonged to the tribe of Reuben. With the Kohathites and the Reubenites camped beside one another on the south side of the tabernacle, it didn't take much for the pride and selfish ambition of these men to infect one another and escalate into this rebellion against Moses. Though they were men of renown and respect, they wanted the greater position and greater prestige that their unholy ambition craved.

One quick side road before we go on: also joining in this rebellion at the outset was On, the son of Peleth, also from the tribe of Reuben. It is interesting to note that only at the introduction of this passage is On mentioned. In the later verses his name is omitted. Is it perhaps because On awoke to his sin of selfish ambition, repented and turned from his sin and left the rebellion? There can be no other explanation; no other reason would have stayed God's hand from the delivery of His judgment that day.

But look now at how Moses responded to the rebellion of these men; "he threw himself down with his face to the ground." He immediately humbled himself before God and before the people and agreed to let God decide what should be done. Do you see the contrast? Selfish ambition will always attempt to exalt itself, whereas surrendered ambition will always humble itself and submit to the will of the Father. Jesus said it best when He said, *"The greatest among you must be a servant. But those who exalt themselves will be humbled, and those who humble themselves will be exalted"* (Matt 23:11-12).

And we read that not only did the Lord respond by slaying these men, He caused the earth to swallow them and all of their possessions. He punished them in a way that was without precedent so that there would be no doubt that they had come under the judgment of God. And it was a fitting judgment that a divide in the earth is what God used to consume those who had attempted to divide the congregation through selfish ambition. God will not allow unholy ambition to stand defiantly before Him.

Unholy ambition will stand with the defiance of Korah, Dathan and Abiram; it will seek its own reward and it will lead to rebellion. Surrendered ambition will lay down before Jesus, surrendered and submitted to the Father; it will seek only Him and His will. Yes, God will humble those with unholy ambition, and He will exalt those whose ambition is to exalt Him.

* * *

23

A SWEET AROMA

But the very next morning the whole community began muttering again against Moses and Aaron, saying, "You two have killed the LORD's people!" As the people gathered to protest to Moses and Aaron, they turned toward the Tabernacle and saw that the cloud had covered it, and the glorious presence of the LORD appeared. Moses and Aaron came and stood at the entrance of the Tabernacle, and the LORD said to Moses, "Get away from these people so that I can instantly destroy them!" But Moses and Aaron fell face down on the ground. And Moses said to Aaron, "Quick, take an incense burner and place burning coals on it from the altar. Lay incense on it and carry it quickly among the people to make atonement for them. The LORD's anger is blazing among them--the plague has already begun." Aaron did as Moses told him and ran out among the people. The plague indeed had already begun, but Aaron burned the incense and made atonement for them. He stood between the living and the dead until the plague was stopped. But 14,700 people died in that plague, in addition to those who had died in the incident involving Korah. Then because the plague had stopped, Aaron returned to Moses at the entrance of the Tabernacle.

Numbers 16:41-50

* * *

You would think that, having just seen God open the earth to swallow Korah, Dathan, Abiram and their possessions, and having just witnessed God's consuming fire destroy the 250 men who sinfully offered offerings of incense to the Lord, the Israelites would be fearful to murmur against Moses and Aaron. But sin so blinds our eyes, deceives our minds and hardens our hearts, that the people did just that – they rebelled against Moses and sinned against God.

i am so grateful to God that He has saved us by His grace and not by our works; or none of us would have a chance of escaping the death and the judgment that we all deserve because of our sin. We must see here the judgment of God that the people of God fell under because of their sin and their rebellion against God. And though we live in the age of grace, our God is the same today as He was yesterday and He will be tomorrow. He has never ignored the sin of His people. He can never turn a blind eye to our sin. The Lord God Jehovah is a just God, and if He were to ignore our sin than He would have to apologize to the 14,700 people who died in that plague. And let's not try and kid ourselves, we are just as rebellious of a people as the Israelites were. We must then get a clear understanding of the grace that you and i are under that keeps us from experiencing that same kind of judgment – the judgment we are due.

Moses told Aaron that day, *"Quick, take an incense burner…and carry it quickly among the people to make atonement for them." And he stood between the living and the dead until the plague was stopped*. The incense symbolized the prayers that were lifted to God, which had been made acceptable before God by the sacrifice of atonement that had been offered. The incense of the golden altar of incense inside the tabernacle was always lit from the fire of the atoning altar of burnt sacrifice outside the tabernacle. You will recall that Aaron's two oldest sons were killed by God for lighting the incense with strange fire. Only the fire from the atoning altar made the offering of the incense acceptable. Because of the sacrifice of atonement for sin, the incense that Aaron burnt before the LORD became a fragrance of the atonement that had been offered for the sin of the people. It became the intercession on their behalf – the sweet aroma of their atonement.

For you and me, the incense symbolizes the intercession that Jesus is making on our behalf that is acceptable to the Father solely on the merit of Christ's atoning death. In fact, the penalty of death has been paid for our sin, but unlike the 14,700 on that day, we have not paid it; it has been paid through the atoning death of Jesus. It is only through His death and resurrection that we can experience the grace of God. It is only through His salvation, received by faith, that we have become the fragrance of Christ. He is the incense and we are His fragrance (2 Cor 2:14-15).

• • •

When once we understand the price He has paid for the atonement of our sin – the price that He has paid so that we can experience His grace – we will then better understand that He has called us to be His sweet aroma. We are to stand like Aaron, not among the living, but between the living and the perishing that through the sweet aroma of Christ in our lives others hear and see Jesus, and the Good News is spread *"like a sweet perfume"*.

Please don't miss this! Throughout our journey, Jesus is interceding for you and for me. By His grace we have not experienced what we deserve; and because of that grace, our lives are to be a sweet aroma offered as an expression of love and worship to Him through which others hear and see Jesus. But fellow sojourner, too many have already perished without having heard or smelled the aroma of His fragrance. Too many are just like we were – blinded, deceived and hardened by sin. Today, no matter where you are in the wilderness, allow the fragrance of Jesus to radiate from your life as a sweet aroma – the aroma of the One who died in order to rescue the perishing.

* * *

24

THE STAFF THAT BLOSSOMS

Then the LORD said to Moses, "Take twelve wooden staffs, one from each of Israel's ancestral tribes, and inscribe each tribal leader's name on his staff. Inscribe Aaron's name on the staff of the tribe of Levi, for there must be one staff for the leader of each ancestral tribe. Put these staffs in the Tabernacle in front of the Ark of the Covenant, where I meet with you. Buds will sprout on the staff belonging to the man I choose. Then I will finally put an end to this murmuring and complaining against you." ...When he went into the Tabernacle of the Covenant the next day, he found that Aaron's staff, representing the tribe of Levi, had sprouted, blossomed, and produced almonds! When Moses brought all the staffs out from the LORD's presence, he showed them to the people. Each man claimed his own staff. And the LORD said to Moses: "Place Aaron's staff permanently before the Ark of the Covenant as a warning to rebels...." Then the people of Israel said to Moses, "We are as good as dead! We are ruined! Everyone who even comes close to the Tabernacle of the LORD dies. We are all doomed!"
Numbers 17:1-5, 8-10, 12-13

* * *

Once and for all God determined to put an end to the controversy over who was to serve as a priest on behalf of the people. Now you would think that the judgments of death that God had already meted out would have settled the issue, but here He used a visual message of life to settle the controversy once and for all.

God instructed Moses to take the staff of the leader of each of the twelve ancestral tribes, together with Aaron's staff, representing the tribe of Levi. These thirteen staffs were then placed overnight in the tabernacle. God promised that buds would sprout from the staff belonging to the man He had chosen to serve as priest.

All of these staffs came from the branches of a tree. They were separated from the tree. They had become dry sticks. A dried separated branch doesn't blossom; it can't bear fruit. Only a living branch, a branch that is connected to the tree, can blossom and bear fruit. From all outside appearance these staffs were very similar. Oh yes, some were probably shorter or longer, thinner or thicker. They may have come from different trees – different wood, so they may have had a slightly different color or appearance. But they had all been turned into staffs by their masters. They all were made for the same purpose – their masters' purpose.

Now, look where the staffs were placed – in the Tabernacle – the earthly dwelling place of the Almighty God; in front of the Ark of the Covenant – the place where God's physical demonstration of His covenant with His people was kept. These were His people under His first covenant – the Law. Now, if we are followers of Jesus, we are His people under His new covenant, a covenant that was made through the shed blood of His only Son – Jesus. That night as the staffs lay in the presence of the almighty God at the feet of His covenant, the one which He chose began to sprout and blossom and bear fruit. In order to blossom, the staff had to be postured in the right place, but it also had to be chosen by God.

That is a picture for us of what Jesus was teaching His disciples in John 15. We have all been fitted for service by our Master. Though we may be shorter or taller, thinner or not so thin, lighter or darker; we have all been uniquely made for our Master's use. He told us – we are branches – we are just like those sticks. He also told us that we must be rightly positioned – in the presence of God, at the feet of Jesus. That is what Jesus was talking about when He said we must abide in Him – surrendered, submitted and sitting at His feet. He told us that the Vinedresser – God the Father – has chosen us. It is because of His choosing that we have been grafted into the Vine. Until then we were dead dry sticks. But now, grafted into the Vine (Jesus), He has made us into living branches; living branches through whom He will bear fruit – just like He did that day through Aaron's staff - fruit that will conspicuously point to the work of the Father.

• • •

No one that day fell down to worship the staff. They knew that the fruit that had been produced, had been produced by God. If we are abiding as His chosen branches, the fruit that is produced will be seen to be His fruit – because dry sticks don't blossom.

It's also interesting to note that there were sprouts, blossoms and almonds all on the staff at the same time. First, that again confirmed the work of God, because even a living branch on its own can only produce one thing at a time. But God was enabling all of those things to be accomplished simultaneously. But secondly, it is a demonstration to us that God will produce a variety of fruit in different stages through a living branch that is rightly connected to the Vine. God will produce fruit through your life that is at varying stages of its development. He is able to do that and to provide just the right nourishment through the branch that the fruit needs for the next stage of its development.

Later we see that God instructed Moses to place the budding branch inside the Ark. The fruit that was on it, remained on it as a lasting reminder to the people of the work of God. The fruit that He produces through our lives will also be fruit that remains for His glory.

As you journey in the wilderness, remember the staff that blossoms is the staff that is chosen by God and rightly positioned before Him and in Him. Be that staff – the staff that blossoms for His glory!

* * *

25

COME TO THE ROCK

In early spring the people of Israel arrived in the wilderness of Zin and camped at Kadesh. While they were there, Miriam died and was buried. There was no water for the people to drink at that place, so they rebelled against Moses and Aaron. The people blamed Moses and said, "We wish we had died in the LORD's presence with our brothers! Did you bring the LORD's people into this wilderness to die, along with all our livestock? Why did you make us leave Egypt and bring us here to this terrible place? This land has no grain, figs, grapes, or pomegranates. And there is no water to drink!" Moses and Aaron turned away from the people and went to the entrance of the Tabernacle, where they fell face down on the ground. Then the glorious presence of the LORD appeared to them, and the LORD said to Moses, "You and Aaron must take the staff and assemble the entire community. As the people watch, command the rock over there to pour out its water. You will get enough water from the rock to satisfy all the people and their livestock." So Moses did as he was told. He took the staff from the place where it was kept before the LORD. Then he and Aaron summoned the people to come and gather at the rock. "Listen, you rebels!" he shouted. "Must we bring you water from this rock?" Then Moses raised his hand and struck the rock twice with the staff, and water gushed out. So all the people and their livestock drank their fill. But the LORD said to Moses and Aaron, "Because you did not trust me enough to demonstrate my holiness to the people of Israel, you will not lead them into the land I am giving them!" This place was known as the waters of Meribah, because it was where the people of Israel argued with the LORD, and where he demonstrated his holiness among them.

Numbers 20:1-13

* * *

The Israelites have now been wandering in the wilderness for thirty-eight years. Their journey of wanderings is drawing to a conclusion. Many of their adult company, including Moses' sister Miriam, have died in the wilderness. A new generation has grown up in the wilderness. Most can barely recall life in Egypt and the pain and the suffering that it entailed. Most cannot recall the sting of the whip of their Egyptian taskmasters. Many cannot remember a day when their diet did not include manna. They have grown up experiencing God's provision from His hand to their mouth and God's presence dwelling among them. Most cannot remember a day when the pillar of cloud by day and the pillar of fire by night have not been before them and among them. Most have buried their parents somewhere in this wilderness. There are still a few men living who led their families in the exodus from Egypt, but most of them who watched in amazement as the Red Sea parted have now died in this wilderness wandering. Most of this company had either not yet been born or were very young when they experienced the miracle at Meribah-Massah in the valley of Rephidim. They did not remember how God had provided water from a rock.

And yet on this day they sounded just like their parents. They murmured, they complained, they rebelled and they blamed Moses. The characters may change among God's people but their fleshly character remains constant. God had delivered them from bondage to deliver them to bounty; it was their sin that had held them captive to the death of the wilderness. How easily they (and we) blame the consequence of their (our) sin on others – including God! And just like their parents, instead of calling upon God for His provision, they complain against God with bitterness. Again instead of sowing seeds of faithfulness, they sow their roots of bitterness and another place in the wilderness is called Meribah (the place of arguing) - this one Meribah-Kadesh.

Moses and Aaron again responded by falling face down on the ground before God. God is going to again prove Himself faithful by meeting their need through a rock. He instructs Moses to stand before the rock and command it to pour forth; and God's provision through it will be sufficient to meet all of their need. And we read that Moses did as he was told. He assembled the people before the rock. He began well. He petitioned the Lord and he set out in faith. But as he stood there, Moses became agitated, anxious and angry with the people and said, "Must we bring you water from this rock?" Then he proceeded to strike the rock twice with his staff. And though the water gushed out and the people drank their fill,

Moses and Aaron were denied the blessing of leading the people into the Promised Land.

What did Moses and Aaron do wrong? Why was the consequence for their actions so huge? Have you ever wondered that if Moses, after faithfully leading the people for almost forty years, gets this punishment for hitting a rock, that you and i have absolutely no chance? God intended to demonstrate His holiness to the people through His servants. Instead His servants revealed their flesh. When Moses asked, "Must we bring you water from this rock?" he kept the attention of the people on Aaron and himself, as if they could actually provide the people with water. He did not turn their attention to God. How often do we stand in the way of allowing God's people to see His Person, His power and His provision and cause them rather to direct their attention to and become focused on the one who was intended to be merely an instrument that God intended to use? In so doing we rob God of the glory that is due Him alone.

God intended to show the people that even the rocks obeyed Him, even when His people did not. God had told them to speak to the rock, instead Moses chose to speak to the people and strike the rock. Moses actions indicated that he thought that the word of God by itself would be insufficient to meet the need. How often do we demonstrate that same unbelief and disobedience through our actions – that the Word of God is not in itself sufficient? Too often we feel that we must add our methods and our manipulations by our own strength. How often do we attempt to draw water from the rock through our programming and our events rather than through the faithful reciting of God's Word?

Throughout the wilderness journey, this people, both this generation and the one before, had continually been guilty of unbelief. God intended to demonstrate the blessings that were available through Him if they would but trust Him. But through his actions, Moses was indicating that God's word alone was not sufficient. That which God had intended to point the people to His faithfulness, would now instead stir their unbelief.

God had called Moses and Aaron to a place of public visibility and He intended to teach the people through them to walk by faith, hope and humility. Moses and Aaron violated that commission through their actions and pointed the people to the same agitation, anxiety and anger that they had demonstrated. God's call to leadership brought with it a calling to greater accountability.

God has placed in our lives His Rock – Jesus – the Rock through which His fountains of blessing will flow, His source of Living Water. All we must do is call upon Him. He has told us that once we drink of Him, we will thirst no more. We will not experience the blessings of the Rock by coming to it in our own strength or our own way. There is only one way to come to the Rock; and that is God's way. We will not enter into His Promised Land any other way. We will not experience the fullness of His blessings any other way. It doesn't matter how good we think we are, or even how good others think we are; we can only come to the Rock God's way. Do not allow this place in your journey to become Meribah, the place of arguing. Come to the Rock and experience the joy and the blessing of His ever-flowing fount. As you do, God will be glorified and His people will be blessed.

* * *

26

THE KING'S HIGHWAY

While Moses was at Kadesh, he sent ambassadors to the king of Edom with this message: "This message is from your relatives, the people of Israel: You know all the hardships we have been through, and that our ancestors went down to Egypt. We lived there a long time and suffered as slaves to the Egyptians. But when we cried out to the LORD, he heard us and sent an angel who brought us out of Egypt. Now we are camped at Kadesh, a town on the border of your land. Please let us pass through your country. We will be careful not to go through your fields and vineyards. We won't even drink water from your wells. We will stay on the king's road and never leave it until we have crossed the opposite border." But the king of Edom said, "Stay out of my land or I will meet you with an army!" The Israelites answered, "We will stay on the main road. If any of our livestock drinks your water, we will pay for it. We only want to pass through your country and nothing else." But the king of Edom replied, "Stay out! You may not pass through our land." With that he mobilized his army and marched out to meet them with an imposing force. Because Edom refused to allow Israel to pass through their country, Israel was forced to turn around.

Numbers 20:14-21

* * *

You will recall that Jacob, son of Isaac, was renamed "Israel" by God at the Jabbok River when he wrestled with God and God blessed him. Jacob's twin brother, Esau, was renamed "Edom" when he traded his birthright to Jacob for a meal of red meat stew. Israel had subsequently usurped Edom's blessing from their father Isaac through deception. The people of Edom and the people of Israel are the descendants of these two twin brothers.

As the people prepared to enter into the Promised Land, they sent greetings to their brothers. It had been over 450 years since the two families had seen one another in the land of Edom. Their reunion had taken place following Jacob's renaming at the Jabbok River. On that occasion, Edom had received his brother Israel with affection and with grace. Since that time the people of Edom had dwelt in this land and established their dominion over it. Israel, on the contrary, had lived as strangers and slaves in a foreign land, and had now wandered in the wilderness for almost forty years. The only land to which they could lay claim, based upon their promise from God, still lay ahead inhabited by others. Thus far the people who had been deceived were fairing much better than those who had received the blessing. Would Edom again be gracious to Israel?

Though God Himself, in a pillar of cloud and fire, was leading the Israelites on their journey, Moses still sought permission from the king of Edom to travel through their land. The Edomites knew that the God of their fathers Abraham and Isaac had delivered the Israelites, had defeated their enemies and had led them through the wilderness; God's deliverance of His people had become notorious. But they also knew of the routing of the Israelites by the Canaanites and the Amalekites when the Israelites had attempted to enter into the Promised Land in defiance of God's command thirty-eight years earlier; the sin of God's people had caused them to become contemptible in the sight of their enemies – even their brothers, the Edomites.

So on this day they sought permission to continue their travel on the king's highway. The king's highway was an old caravan route from Egypt through the Sinai Peninsula into the eastern lands of the Edomites, the Moabites and the Ammonites and the eastern borders of the Mediterranean Sea. It was the most direct route from Kadesh into the Promised Land. But the king of Edom denied entry to the people of God. The King of kings was leading His people along the king's highway, but the king of Edom denied His people entry. The king even assembled his armies and rallied an imposing force to demonstrate his resolve. (Think about the foolishness of that move; God had single-handedly destroyed the Egyptian army, the most formidable army of its day, and this display of bravado made no impression on the King of kings.)

• • •

i am reminded of the day that the King of kings had set His face toward Jerusalem (Luke 9:51-56). In His path was a Samaritan village. He sent messengers ahead to make arrangements, but they returned with the message that the village had denied Jesus entry. Though two of His disciples wanted Him to destroy the village by fire, Jesus turned and went another way. What was the consequence to that Samaritan village for denying entry to Jesus that day? They missed experiencing His Person, His presence and His power. Those that were sick did not experience His healing, those that were burdened did not experience His comfort and compassion, and those that were sinners (and that would be all of them) did not experience His salvation and His mercy. You see, the price for failing to allow Him passage was greater than any immediate destruction they could have experienced.

The same is true of the Edomites. By failing to allow God's people passage through the land, they too missed out on the blessing of helping God's people, and most importantly, they too missed out on experiencing the Person, the presence and the power of the Lord God Jehovah as He led His people. God chose not to destroy the Edomites that day; He chose to lead His people in another direction. (Years later they would be defeated by the Israelites under the leadership of King David and made subjects of his kingdom.) God allowed His children to be turned from the king's highway that day. In His sovereignty He had purpose and intentions along an alternate route. The king of Edom did not thwart the purpose of the Sovereign and Almighty God any more than the Samaritan village thwarted Jesus; but in their resistance they missed out on the blessings of God.

As God leads you on your journey through this wilderness, remember that you are walking on The King's Highway; and the King of kings is leading you. Do not be discouraged if you are turned from your course; your God is still in control. He will allow others around you to exercise their free will, and in so doing, He will allow them to miss out on the blessing of seeing you pass through their way. But remember, His will and His purpose will still be accomplished. Even if He leads you to make a turn to the right or the left, keep walking on the King's Highway – His Highway leads to victory!

* * *

27

PASSING THE BATON

Then the LORD said to Moses and Aaron at Mount Hor on the border of the land of Edom, "The time has come for Aaron to join his ancestors in death. He will not enter the land I am giving the people of Israel, because the two of you rebelled against my instructions concerning the waters of Meribah. Now take Aaron and his son Eleazar up Mount Hor. There you will remove Aaron's priestly garments and put them on Eleazar, his son. Aaron will die there and join his ancestors." So Moses did as the LORD commanded. The three of them went up Mount Hor together as the whole community watched. At the summit, Moses removed the priestly garments from Aaron and put them on Eleazar, Aaron's son. Then Aaron died there on top of the mountain, and Moses and Eleazar went back down. When the people realized that Aaron had died, all Israel mourned for him thirty days.
Numbers 20:23-29

* * *

Moses experienced the death of his sister Miriam at the beginning of Numbers chapter 20, and here, at its conclusion, he experiences the passing of his brother Aaron. The baton of servant leadership is being passed from one generation to the next. Even journeys through the wilderness can encompass more than one generation. God has been at work since before the beginning of time to accomplish His purpose and He has given men and women an opportunity to be a part of His plan for a season and a time throughout the ages. And though His purpose will be without end, our time and season will come to a conclusion.

. . .

Aaron had been preparing his son Eleazar for this day. He had taught him through the Words of God as conveyed through Moses, he had taught him through his actions – both the good and the bad, and he had taught him by allowing him to assume greater responsibility along the way. And on this day Moses removed the priestly garments from Aaron and put them on Eleazar. The transition now being complete, Aaron died peacefully and was buried on the summit of the mount.

In Ecclesiastes we read, *"There is a time for everything, a season for every activity under heaven"* (Eccl 3:1). Every activity is a part of God's grand plan, either through His perfect will or His permissive will. God had planted the seed of His plan for His people at the garden when He told the serpent, *"And I will put enmity between you and the woman, and between your seed and her Seed; He shall bruise your head, and you shall bruise His heel"* (Gen 3:15 NKJ). His plan involved a people that He would raise up through Abraham, through Isaac and through Jacob. He would lead them into Egypt where they would multiply into a great nation. After 400 years He would deliver them from their taskmasters and lead them through the wilderness to His Promised Land. Despite the sinfulness of this people, He would continue to be faithful to them, delivering them, protecting them and drawing them back to Himself. Through this people a Child would be born and a Son given – Jesus of Nazareth – to save all peoples from the penalty of sin. God would raise up a people that would proclaim His Good News throughout Jerusalem, Judea, Samaria and the ends of the earth. Across the centuries God would call men, women and children to be a part of His Story, the Story of His glory. The cast of characters would continuously change, but God's plan of redemption would be constant and continuous. It is God that chooses the cast of characters. It is God that makes the assignments; it is He that determines the length of their performance. Often He changes our assignments throughout the journey, leading us to different places of service for different seasons. And ultimately, unless Jesus returns to rapture His church beforehand, He will call us to heaven through physical death, ending our season of physical service, just as He has with those that have gone before us.

It was God's time in the season of His story and in the life of Aaron. Aaron was far from perfect in his obedience to God. In fact it was because of his disobedience that God prevented him from entering the Promised Land with the people. But Aaron had carried the mantle of leadership of God's people with his brother Moses. Though we could quickly enumerate his failures, don't disregard his faithfulness. For over thirty-eight years he was the high priest interceding before God for the people. On many occasions he interceded for God's grace and mercy on the people's behalf. Aaron was now over 120 years old. Physically and emotionally, he was tired. He had been faithful to train the leadership that would take his place. And now it was time for him to step from this earthly assignment to the next one that God had for him. The people could grieve for his passing, but they could not have regret for his passing, and neither can we. Though he didn't enter the Promised Land, he entered into a place far greater – the Kingdom of Heaven.

Throughout your life and your journey, God will reassign you to different places of service – for His time and His season. Be mindful of three things in the process. First, make sure that it is He who is making the assignments. We are not called to make our own assignments; we are called to follow Him. Do not go anywhere that God is not leading you to go; and do not stay anywhere once He has led you to go. Second, following the counsel of the Apostle Paul to a man by the name of Archippus, *"Be sure to carry out the work the Lord gave you"* (Col 4:17). Be faithful to carry out all that God has set before you, including the preparation of those that He places in your path to continue the work. Third, hold onto the garment of service that He has clothed you in lightly. The garments are not yours, they are His. He has placed them on you for this season, but in His time you must be prepared to relinquish them to His next servant.

God has placed you on this journey through the wilderness because He is leading you from one place of service to another. But He also has you in a place of service while you are on this journey. Be faithful to carry out the work the Lord gave you for whatever time He has given it to you. And then when that time is concluded allow Him to lead you to His next assignment in peace. As you remove the garments of service, there will be a grief – for you will be saying goodbye to those that you love – but there will be no regret – for God has called you to pass the baton.

* * *

28

HORMAH REVISITED

The Canaanite king of Arad, who lived in the Negev, heard that the Israelites were approaching on the road to Atharim. So he attacked the Israelites and took some of them as prisoners. Then the people of Israel made this vow to the LORD: "If you will help us conquer these people, we will completely destroy all their towns." The LORD heard their request and gave them victory over the Canaanites. The Israelites completely destroyed them and their towns, and the place has been called Hormah ever since.

Numbers 21:1-3

* * *

The men of Arad were assembled in the Negev. The city of Arad was located at the southern boundary of Canaan, and the Negev was the southern desert wilderness that divided the land of Canaan from the Sinai Peninsula. You will recall that the twelve spies had journeyed through the Negev when they explored the Promised Land some thirty-nine years earlier. You will also recall the rebellion against God by the people when they heard the report of the spies. God commanded that they should wander this wilderness for forty years. But you will also recall that they attempted then to enter the Promised Land in disobedience to God. They went forward without God and were soundly defeated by the armies of the Amalekites and the Canaanites. You may recall that the defeat took place at Hormah.

The men of Arad were probably a part of the Canaanite army that defeated the Israelites that day. i can just imagine the victory celebration of the Amalekites and the Canaanites. They had heard of this people and how their God had delivered them from Egypt. They had heard of the defeat of the Egyptian army at the hand of their God. Their Amalekite brothers had in fact experienced defeat themselves at the hands of these Israelites on that day when Aaron and Hur had upheld Moses' raised arms. So imagine their relief and their elation when they routed this people that day at Hormah. Had they heard properly? Was this really this people who followed this God who was to be feared? Or were the gods of the Canaanites greater than the God of Israel? There was no question that it had been an easy victory; those Israelites were routed that day. It had taken very little effort on the part of the Canaanites. No big deal!

The king of Arad had been a youth when the armies defeated these Israelites. He, like most of the men under his command, had heard the story retold time and again about how their armies had crushed these upstarts wandering in the wilderness and their God. A few of the men that had been young men in the army that day were in fact a part of this group now gathered in the Negev. And as the Aradites heard that the Israelites were again headed in their direction, these men who had been young, looked forward to that second taste of victory, and stirred the hearts of the men of their company.

Thirty-nine years ago there had been men from other cities of Canaan that had been a part of their force, but given how handily they had won on that day, there was no need to call any other men to join them. Besides, these were the men of Arad. Arad was a fugitive city. It was inhabited by the toughest and the meanest. They had been fighting to survive for as long as they could remember. These were some bad dudes – and they didn't need anybody to help them fight these "wimps in the wilderness"! And this was the opportunity for the king of Arad to make a name for himself. No longer would people speak of his father's victory; now they would speak of his. Are you getting the picture? Do you understand the arrogance with which these people chose to attack the Israelites? It was a lot like the arrogance with which the Israelites approached them the first time in disobedience to God.

But this time, the Israelites called out to God and He heard them; and He went before them. You see the pagan army hadn't realized that God hadn't gone before the Israelites the first time; but they were about to experience the mighty hand of the Lord God Jehovah. God gave them victory that day. It was victory so complete that the army and their cities were utterly and completely destroyed – nothing was left standing. That's why the area was named Hormah. Hormah means "complete destruction."

That is the story of Hormah revisited. The first time, without God, the Israelites had been defeated; the second time, with God, their enemy had been completely destroyed. So what is the lesson of Hormah revisited for us on our journey? Apart from our God, we are at the mercy of our enemies. We will experience defeat, ridicule and destruction. Do not underestimate the power of the enemy. On your own, you will not be able to escape defeat. BUT, there is no enemy that God is not able to utterly destroy. Don't miss this – in verse 3 we read, "God gave them victory". He delivered the people into their hands. They didn't attain victory; God gave it to them. And He will give us victory over any and every enemy we encounter if we will but walk with Him – in obedience to Him, by His side, following His steps. And that which God defeats He utterly destroys.

No matter what you are facing today in your journey, walk in the victory of Hormah revisited!

* * *

29

IT ALL STARTED WITH A LITTLE DETOUR

Then the people of Israel set out from Mount Hor, taking the road to the Red Sea to go around the land of Edom. But the people grew impatient along the way, and they began to murmur against God and Moses. "Why have you brought us out of Egypt to die here in the wilderness?" they complained. "There is nothing to eat here and nothing to drink. And we hate this wretched manna!" So the LORD sent poisonous snakes among them, and many of them were bitten and died. Then the people came to Moses and cried out, "We have sinned by speaking against the LORD and against you. Pray that the LORD will take away the snakes." So Moses prayed for the people. Then the LORD told him, "Make a replica of a poisonous snake and attach it to the top of a pole. Those who are bitten will live if they simply look at it!" So Moses made a snake out of bronze and attached it to the top of a pole. Whenever those who were bitten looked at the bronze snake, they recovered!

Numbers 21:4-9

* * *

The other night as i was driving to pick up my son, i encountered an intersection that had been closed overnight to accommodate work on a new overpass. My only option was to retrace my steps in the opposite direction and make a detour around the blocked intersection. It was late and i was ready to be in bed; and i was not a happy camper. i could not get over how inconsiderate this construction company was – the miles they were adding to my journey, my time they were wasting and ultimately the rest deprivation they were causing me. And the further out of my way i had to drive, the more agitated i got. To a much greater degree that is what had happened to the Israelites. Because of the refusal of the Edomites to grant them access through their land, the Israelites were now headed south toward the Red Sea in a giant detour, when they should have been going north toward the Promised Land. And just like i was in the car the other night, they began to murmur. It was one of those murmurs that the further you go, the more agitated you get, and the more things you find to become agitated about. i mean the further i drove, my murmuring expanded beyond the "inconsiderate" construction company to the "inconsiderate" man who was driving two miles below the speed limit in front of me, to my loving "inconsiderate" wife who was asleep in our bed back home, to my "inconsiderate" son who just wanted to go bowling with his friends. Are you getting the picture? i know you have never experienced anything like this, or felt that way yourself! Well for the Israelites, it started with the "inconsiderate" Edomites, and grew to this rocky, sandy wilderness, to the absence of a varied diet, to "this wretched manna"! "So the Lord sent poisonous snakes among them!" Boy, am i glad that there weren't any poisonous snakes around the other night!

You see, my agitation the other night really didn't have anything to do with my "inconsiderate" son, or my "inconsiderate" wife, or the "inconsiderate" driver, or even the "inconsiderate" construction company; it all had to do with me, my response and what was in my heart. And the issue that day as the Israelites traveled from Mount Hor didn't have anything to do with manna, or their diet, or the wilderness, or even the Edomites; it had to do with what was in their hearts. When will we learn that other people or circumstances cannot "make" us angry or agitated or bitter or whatever. That person or those people or that circumstance may have jostled our cup, but whatever came spilling out was in there to begin with; that anger, that bitterness, etc. was there long before we encountered this person or circumstance. God was dealing with what was in the people's hearts that day, and had been in their hearts for quite some time.

So He sent the snakes. It is interesting to note that the wilderness was and always had been infested with those snakes. In Deuteronomy we read, *"Do not forget that he led you through the great and terrifying wilderness with poisonous snakes and scorpions, where it was so hot and dry"* (Deut 8:15) To this point, for almost forty years God had protected His people from them, but on this day He allowed the snakes to invade the camp. The anger and bitterness of their hearts was met with the bite of the poisonous snakes, all of which was there in the wilderness long before this day. That happens in our lives too; anger or bitterness or sin of any kind that remains unchecked in our hearts, even if it has lied dormant for some time, will eventually poison our entire self – physically, emotionally, mentally and spiritually. It will literally eat us up from the inside out. Now before you start jumping to the defense of the Israelites and wondering why did God zap them with snakes "just for murmuring", God's plan here was for their cleansing and their redemption. Yes, God would not tolerate their sin; and the price of their sin was death; but God made a way in the wilderness for them to be cleansed – He made a way for the redemption of their sin.

God instructed Moses to make a bronze snake and lift it up on a pole above the people, and He told the people that those who turned toward it and looked upon it would recover. Now you have to admit that from a human perspective the plan doesn't make much sense. First, it's too simple. All they had to do was look at the bronze snake. They didn't have to go through protracted acts of contrition; all they had to do was turn toward it, believing that God would enable them to be made whole because of it. i wonder how many died because they wouldn't turn to look because it seemed too simple to be true. Second, the cure was formed in the same shape as the cause. It reminds me of the words of the apostle Paul, "*He sent his own Son in a human body like ours, except that ours are sinful. God destroyed sin's control over us by giving his Son as a sacrifice for our sins*" (Rom 8:3). Third, the bronze snake was lifted up before all the people. And, yes, Jesus was lifted up as the redemption for all, so that whoever turns to Him might be saved. That bronze snake was a picture of the incarnate Lord Jesus.

Jesus said, "*And when I am lifted up on the cross, I will draw everyone to myself*" (John 12:32). Jesus was lifted up for our salvation, our cleansing from sin, our sanctification. As children of the Living God, He has permitted the detours in our journey to surface the dross in our hearts. We must not let that dross remain and fester and poison us just like the bites of those snakes. Rather, we must turn to the One who has been lifted up and experience the cleansing, the healing and the life that only He can bring. Yes, it all started with a little detour, but even that detour will lead to His cleansing, His healing and His forgiveness if we will but turn to Him.

* * *

30

THE LESSONS OF THE DETOUR

The Israelites traveled next to Oboth and camped there. Then they went on to Iye-abarim, in the wilderness on the eastern border of Moab. From there they traveled to the valley of Zered Brook and set up camp. Then they moved to the far side of the Arnon River, in the wilderness adjacent to the territory of the Amorites. The Arnon is the boundary line between the Moabites and the Amorites. For this reason The Book of the Wars of the LORD speaks of "the town of Waheb in the area of Suphah, and the ravines; and the Arnon River and its ravines, which extend as far as the settlement of Ar on the border of Moab." From there the Israelites traveled to Beer, which is the well where the LORD said to Moses, "Assemble the people, and I will give them water." There the Israelites sang this song: "Spring up, O well! Yes, sing about it! Sing of this well, which princes dug, which great leaders hollowed out with their scepters and staffs." Then the Israelites left the wilderness and proceeded on through Mattanah, Nahaliel, and Bamoth. Then they went to the valley in Moab where Pisgah Peak overlooks the wasteland.

Numbers 21:10-20

* * *

As we read through this passage, we can easily gloss over the travelogue of places that are hard to pronounce in our attempt to get to the "good stuff". If we do, we will miss some of the most important lessons that God would teach us in the wilderness. Let's not forget what Paul told Timothy, "*All Scripture is inspired by God and is useful to teach us what is true and to make us realize what is wrong in our lives. It straightens us out and teaches us to do what is right. It is God's way of preparing us in every way, fully equipped for every good thing God wants us to do"* (2 Tim 3:16-17).

This journey around the Land of Edom was approximately one hundred miles and took the Israelites six days, traveling approximately sixteen miles per day. They now stood at the edge of the Promised Land. Despite the Edomites' refusal to permit them passage, the Israelites were now right where they needed to be. The first lesson we might have overlooked is that the enemy may sometimes cause us to detour, but he can never prevent our arrival. Do not lose sight that God is sovereign even in the detours, and as we'll see in a minute, God has blessings in store for us even along the way of the detours. As we journey through the wilderness, we too will encounter detours placed in our path by the enemy. Remember Joseph's admonition to his brothers that what they meant for evil, God intended for good (Gen 50:20). God will lead you through the detour and you will arrive at His intended destination.

Moses takes a moment in verse 14 and refers to "The Book of the Wars of the Lord". This is the book that God instructed Moses to keep after His defeat of the Amalekites (Ex 17:14). It was a record of the victories that God accomplished on behalf of His people. The second lesson we might have overlooked is the reminder that we must keep a written record of the victories God accomplishes along the way. We must take time to celebrate the favor and the victories of God, preserving them in writing for our future recollection, as well as for the generations that follow. We must record, and in that manner preserve, an account of what He has done, where He has done it and when He has done it. As we have seen time and again in the account of the Israelites, they were quick to forget the goodness and the graciousness of God. But, guess what – so are you and I! We must be faithful to record, review and recite the victories of God in days past; and allow those to provoke us to even greater faith in His Person, His promises and His purpose in the days ahead.

This passage begins at a place called Oboth, which means "water skins". God provided them with water sufficient for the detour. But now six days later as they arrive in Beer their water bottles are empty; the water supply is exhausted. And do you know what the Israelites did not do? For the first time in forty years when their water supply was exhausted – they did not complain! In verse 17 the people look to the Lord God Jehovah to see how He is going to provide. Finally, they got it – at least for now! God gathered the people and He instructed the seventy elders to place their staffs in the ground. Notice He didn't have Moses strike the rock, or even speak to it; as a matter of fact, He didn't even work through Moses for this miracle; He worked through the seventy elders. And as they placed their staffs in the ground, water sprang forth, and there was more than enough for the people and their animals. The third lesson we might have overlooked is the reminder that God will rarely meet similar needs in the same way; but He will always meet the need. As God meets the need, it will be in ways that bring glory to Him; and it will often be in ways that are above and beyond anything that we could hope or ask. One pattern will always be consistent – the people prayed according to God's will, He heard them and He answered. And as He answered, the people responded with joy and thankfulness.

The detour ended with the people crossing from the wilderness into the valley of Moab. The fourth lesson we might have overlooked is the reminder that our Lord is our Shepherd and He will lead us to the green pastures and the quiet waters. He knew what the people had need of before they even asked, and as the Good Shepherd He was, and is, faithful to provide it. No matter where you are in your journey, even if there is only desert wilderness in sight, be confident; He will lead you to those green pastures and quiet waters.

i don't know what detour you might have encountered on your journey through the wilderness; but don't overlook the lessons He would teach you through it. These lessons are as much a part of His preparation as any other you will encounter. Heed the lessons of the detour.

* * *

31

ONE DOWN, FIVE TO GO

The Israelites now sent ambassadors to King Sihon of the Amorites with this message: "Let us travel through your land. We will stay on the king's road until we have crossed your territory. We will not trample your fields or touch your vineyards or drink your well water." But King Sihon refused to let them cross his land. Instead, he mobilized his entire army and attacked Israel in the wilderness, engaging them in battle at Jahaz. But the Israelites slaughtered them and occupied their land from the Arnon River to the Jabbok River. They went only as far as the Ammonite border because the boundary of the Ammonites was fortified. So Israel captured all the towns of the Amorites and settled in them, including the city of Heshbon and its surrounding villages. Heshbon had been the capital of King Sihon of the Amorites. So the people of Israel occupied the territory of the Amorites.

Numbers 21:21-26, 31

* * *

Do you remember God's promise from the beginning of the journey? God promised the people, "For my angel will go before you and bring you into the land of the Amorites, Hittites, Perizzites, Canaanites, Hivites, and Jebusites, so you may live there. And I will destroy them" (Ex 23:23) Note that the Amorites were the first on that list of six. But still as the Israelites approached the Amorites, they did so as gentlemen. They did not swagger and address them with arrogance. Though they had the assurance of victory from God, they sent a peaceable message to King Sihon. We, too, are to be ambassadors of peace to a world that is full of turmoil. Though we have been assured of victory over whatever this world puts before us, we are to do so in a spirit of peace and humility. More often than not, our message is compromised by an attitude of arrogance. i am mindful that our Savior – God incarnate – put on the towel of a servant; He humbled Himself. We must heed this lesson: never to compromise our message, but we must present it in the attitude of a servant – a servant of the Master.

Do not be surprised if your peaceable message is responded to with an unpeaceable reply. The Israelites had received a similar reply from the King of Edom; and his reply had resulted in a detour. But King Sihon's unpeaceable reply was followed by an unprovoked attack. God never promised His people that their message would be peaceably received and He never promised them that they would not be attacked. And He has never given us that promise. As a matter of fact, He told us that as His followers, we will experience the persecution of this world. But He assured us that the persecution would lead to an opportunity of testimony to His glory (Luke 21:13). It will lead to His ultimate victory. This provocation from the King of the Amorites led to just such a victory.

The Lord defeated the Amorites, and the Israelites occupied the land from the Arnon River to the Jabbok River. It is interesting to me that the first land God gave His children included that place where Jacob wrestled with God (the Jabbok River), where God changed his name to Israel and blessed him. That same blessing was now continuing to his descendants almost five hundred years later. You see, **the victory God gave the Israelites put them in possession of the land; but it was the promise that God gave them that assured them of that victory**. We must walk with that same confidence in the assurance of our promise from Him, even when we have yet to experience its possession.

Why did the Israelites not cross the border into the land of the Ammonites? First, God did not lead them beyond that border because, second, He did not promise them beyond that border. Grab that principle – **God will never lead you beyond the boundaries of His promise**! You will possess ALL of the land within the boundaries of His promise, but you must never step beyond the boundaries of His promise. It is interesting to note that God assembled all of the land that He promised the Israelites into the hands of the Amorites, Hittites, Perizzites, Canaanites, Hivites, and Jebusites. Matthew Henry wrote, *"All that God intended for His chosen people He put into the possession of the nations that were to be driven out."* The land God was now giving to the Israelites had at one time been possessed by the Moabites. But the Amorites had taken the land from the Moabites. God had told the Israelites that they could never possess any land belonging to Moab, the descendants of Abraham's nephew Lot (Deut 2:9). But God intended Israel to have this particular portion of land, so He had allowed the Amorites to take it from Moab. In essence they became trustees of the land for the Israelites – until it was God's time for them to possess it. Be mindful that God will accomplish His purpose according to His promise in His time and it will never violate His Word.

Though their journey was far from over, they began to inhabit the land of God's promise that day. There were still many miles to be traveled and battles to be fought. There was still much land to be possessed and obstacles to overcome. But on that day, God reaffirmed His promise – and there was one down, five to go.

i don't know where you are on your journey through the wilderness, or how long you have been wandering. But God's promise today is as true as it was at the beginning of your journey. Continue confidently, even if you have not yet begun to possess any of the land. Allow God to embolden you with the confidence that He gave the Israelites that day – the confidence of "one down, five to go".

* * *

32

HAVE YOU ENCOUNTERED ANY GIANTS LATELY?

Then they turned and marched toward Bashan, but King Og of Bashan and all his people attacked them at Edrei. The LORD said to Moses, "Do not be afraid of him, for I have given you victory over Og and his entire army, giving you all his land. You will do the same to him as you did to King Sihon of the Amorites, who ruled in Heshbon." And Israel was victorious and killed King Og, his sons, and his subjects; not a single survivor remained. Then Israel occupied their land.
Numbers 21:33-35

* * *

Have you encountered any giants in the wilderness lately? Giants are those enemies or obstacles that you encounter that just seem insurmountable and undefeatable. They are larger than life and can intimidate the stew out of you. They stand between you and the realization of the promise that God has given you; and they pride themselves on confronting people that are journeying through the wilderness. Do not think they are an illusion. Not only do they look like they could defeat you, they have their hearts set on doing just that.

Meet Og. Og was another Amorite king who lived in the city of Bashan. Og had heard about the defeat of Sihon, king of Heshbon; but that was Sihon, and he was Og. We get a little more insight into Og in Deuteronomy where we read, "*Incidentally, King Og of Bashan was the last of the giant Rephaites. His iron bed was more than thirteen feet long and six feet wide. It can still be seen in the Ammonite city of Rabbah*" (Deut 3:11). i like the fact that the entire verse is in parentheses and begins with the word "incidentally". Can't you just hear it? "Og and his entire army are attacking; and, oh by the way, do you know why Og has a bed that is thirteen feet long?" Og is twelve to thirteen feet tall! "Don't worry; you can't miss Og, he's the big dude on the right that eats people like you and me for breakfast." My head would barely reach his kneecaps – we're talking a BIG guy! Og was the last of this race of giants that had inhabited this land since before the days of Abraham. This whole region of Bashan, Gilead and Argob was called the land of giants. It was this region and these people that the twelve spies had spoken of when they had given their report thirty-eight years prior. And i will admit, it is one thing to hear about the giants, it is quite another to encounter them personally.

Sometimes i enjoy when the Bible is silent on a point. Here for example, King Og is attacking and the Lord said to Moses, "Do not be afraid of him." Don't you wonder what Moses said to God before God told him not to be afraid? i personally think he was standing there with wide eyes and his mouth hanging open. i mean, Moses had seen Pharaoh and knew the Egyptian traditions that taught that the Pharaoh had hung the sun and the moon, and he knew better. But Og LOOKED like he had hung the sun and the moon. He was an intimidating giant! Moses looked at himself, then he looked at the other Israelite men, then he looked at the giant and he thought to himself, "There is no way we can beat this guy".

But then he turned to God and God said, "Don't be afraid of him", (and if you'll permit my paraphrase) "Og's head doesn't even reach My kneecaps". "I have given you victory over the Amorites, and that includes Og and his entire army. And you will not just defeat Og, you will utterly destroy him." And not a survivor remained.

In that same passage in Deuteronomy we read that Og's iron bed could still be seen in the city of Rabbah. Do you know why they kept that bed? As a reminder that there is no enemy big enough or giant tall enough to intimidate God. You see, the Israelites stood there looking up at Og and saw "O-G", the giant; however, God looked down at Og from His perspective and saw "G-O", the next step in the path to God's glory.

The lesson the Israelites learned that day was, and the lesson that we must learn today is, that God will take the "Og's" in our path and turn them into "Go's". God has permitted every circumstance and every obstacle that you encounter along the way to be in your path. God didn't will for Og to attack the Israelites; but He knew that Og was going to attack. And God intended to use that attack to His glory. Remember that there is no giant or obstacle that you will encounter in your path today or throughout the journey that God is not able to overcome. Get your eyes off the giant and turn them to God. Also bear in mind that Og was probably not the only giant on the field that day. His army was probably composed of many giants. Not only does their size not intimidate God, neither does their number. If God promised to defeat the Amorites so that you can inhabit the land, He didn't just mean the little bitty ones; He meant ALL of them, including the Og's. Watch how God leads you to victory!

* * *

33

CURSINGS FOR SALE?

Then the people of Israel traveled to the plains of Moab.... Balak son of Zippor, the Moabite king, knew what the Israelites had done to the Amorites. And ... he and his people were terrified. ... So Balak, king of Moab, sent messengers to Balaam son of Beor.... He sent this message to request that Balaam come to help him: "A vast horde of people has arrived from Egypt. They cover the face of the earth and are threatening me. Please come and curse them for me because they are so numerous. Then perhaps I will be able to conquer them and drive them from the land. I know that blessings fall on the people you bless. I also know that the people you curse are doomed." Balak's messengers, officials of both Moab and Midian, set out and took money with them to pay Balaam to curse Israel.... "Stay here overnight," Balaam said. "In the morning I will tell you whatever the LORD directs me to say." So the officials from Moab stayed there with Balaam. That night God came to Balaam.... "Do not go with them," God told Balaam. "You are not to curse these people, for I have blessed them!" The next morning Balaam got up and told Balak's officials, "Go on home! The LORD will not let me go with you."

Numbers 22:1-13

* * *

Fresh on the heels of their victory over the Amorites, the Israelites traveled to the plains of Moab on the east side of the Jordan River. News of the Israelites' utter destruction of the Amorites had reached the people of Moab. The news did not cause grief in the hearts of the Moabites; the Amorites had been the enemy of Moab. As a matter of fact, you may recall from our look at the defeat of the Amorites in Numbers 21, that they had seized a portion of the land they possessed from the Moabites. They had taken it by defeating Zippor, who was at that time king of the Moabites. And now Balak, Zippor's son, is king, and the memory of his father's defeat at the hands of the Amorites was still very fresh in his mind, and in the minds of the people. They all knew that the Israelites had handily defeated the Amorites. This did not bode well for the Moabites. They were terrified that these Israelites would now finish the job started by the Amorites and take all of their remaining land. They knew that militarily they could not defeat the Israelites, because they knew that God went before these people. (Would that God's presence was that conspicuous in the lives of His people today!)

The Moabites, though descendants of Abraham's nephew Lot (Gen 19:36-37), did not worship the One true God; they worshipped many gods. But they knew of this God of Abraham, and they knew that He went before this people.

As we have already seen, God had forbidden the Israelites from harassing the Moabites or provoking them to war. God was not going to give the Israelites any of the land that the Moabites possessed (Gen 13:10-11; Deut 2:9). The Moabites were not under any danger of attack from the Israelites; they truly were under the protection of God from His people. But though Balak knew of God, he did not know God and he did not know of His promises. Thus Balak, king of Moab, was terrified, as were his people, and he devised his own plan to protect his people.

In order for his plan to work, Balak needed to enlist the help of the Midianites. (Again, by way of background, you will recall that the Midianites were also descendants of Abraham; Midian was his fourth son by Keturah. You will also recall that the Midianites were known for their skill as merchantmen – as men of business. Though Moses had married a Midianite, Zipporah, and his father-in-law, Jethro, was a prince and priest of Midian; this group did not follow Jethro, and they had no affection for Moses or for these Israelites.) Balak convinced the Midianites that the Israelites would destroy all of the natural resources of Moab and Midian – and appealed to the Midianites' pocketbooks that this would "not be good for business."

Having now appealed to their compelling financial interests, he enlisted their support in contacting (and probably help to underwrite) a Midianite soothsayer that he had heard of, by the name of Balaam. Balaam had developed the reputation that whomever he cursed would be cursed, and whomever he blessed would be blessed. And apparently Balaam had developed a lucrative business (remember, he was a Midianite!) of blessings and cursings. The messengers, representing both Moab and Midian, came to Balaam with money in hand. Does it make you wonder what the price was for a cursing in 1401 B.C.? Well, whatever they brought, it was sufficient enough for Balaam to inquire of God.

Now it is important to understand that Balaam inquired of God, not out of motivation to know God's will, nor out of a motivation to know God, but out of a motivation whether or not to take the money. Do not attribute his inquiry of God to anything noble; Balaam was motivated by greed! And surprisingly enough, God answered him. God told him, "These are My people. I have blessed them and you are not to curse them."

Please don't miss this. Balaam was not a servant of God; he was a soothsayer. But he knew that he had heard from God. When God desires to make His will known, He will do so – and He will do so in any manner He desires – even through a profit-seeking soothsayer (but don't go there looking for His answers!). And this soothsayer who made a living from blessing and cursing was not going to cross the Lord God Jehovah, at least not for the amount of money Balak was offering. So he sent the messengers back to Balak with his refusal to help.

We're going to pick up with this story in the next chapter, but we need to seize the lessons that have unfolded thus far. All of this plotting and conniving by Balak was totally unnecessary. He and the Moabites were already protected by God – they just didn't know it. He developed this elaborate scheme to seek the cooperation of the Midianites and Balaam, when all he needed to do was inquire directly of the Lord God Jehovah. i am mindful that the world, and too often even we as believers, will seek answers from everybody else, but we will not seek the Lord. He is the One with the answer, and His is the only answer that matters; and yet, we'll seek everybody else and every other thing before we'll inquire of him.

We'll see later that Balak's deceptions eventually cost his people their land – land that would have otherwise been protected by God. His failure to seek God, like ours when we fail to do so, bears a price; and it will be a price that we cannot afford to pay. You see our failure to seek God and go His way will always cost us. Remember what the wages of sin are?

The third thing we need to see here is that the Israelites were oblivious to it all! Praise God they were not worrying, fretting, murmuring or complaining! They were right where God had led them in the center of His presence and His will. And when we are there – there is no safer place on the face of the earth. God had blessed His people; and those whom God blesses, no man can curse. That which God has given, no man can take away unless God permits it! Remember that today as you journey in this wilderness – if God has led you where you are today, you, too, are in the center of His presence and His will. No enemy (even the ones you don't know about) can harm you. You are protected by His power, you are enveloped by His presence, and you are blessed by His Person. No cursings are for sale!

* * *

34

WHAT IS YOUR ANSWER?

So the Moabite officials returned to King Balak and reported, "Balaam refused to come with us." Then Balak tried again. This time he sent a larger number of even more distinguished officials than those he had sent the first time. They went to Balaam and gave him this message: "This is what Balak son of Zippor says: Please don't let anything stop you from coming. I will pay you well and do anything you ask of me. Just come and curse these people for me!" But Balaam answered them, "Even if Balak were to give me a palace filled with silver and gold, I would be powerless to do anything against the will of the LORD my God. But stay here one more night to see if the LORD has anything else to say to me." That night God came to Balaam and told him, "Since these men have come for you, get up and go with them. But be sure to do only what I tell you to do."

Numbers 22:14-20

* * *

Well, you have to give Balak credit; he did not give up easily. Balak would not take "No" for an answer. If only the people of God had that much tenacity! That tenacity flowed out of Balak's desperation. Perhaps our lack of tenacity flows out of our lack of desperation – desperation for God. Balak was desperate for an answer. He had looked at the problem that he and his people faced, and he was convinced that this was the only solution. Military might wouldn't work; the defeat of the Amorites had proven that. Compromise wouldn't work; it would certainly cost him part of his kingdom, and that was unacceptable. What about calling upon the Lord God Jehovah directly? That possibility never entered his radar screen. Though their father, Lot, and his firstborn daughter, by whom Moab was born, had been rescued from the destruction of Sodom and Gomorrah by the God of Abraham and led by Him to safety; and though the land they now inhabited had been given to them by this same God, the Moabites had turned from Him many years before and turned to the gods of this world. Balak had become blinded to the truth, and the only solution he saw was through divination and soothsaying; and Balaam was his man. No, he wouldn't give up; to do so would be to condemn himself and his people to defeat. Balak was a desperate man.

Balaam's reputation was obviously one of profit and not principle. So Balak decided to raise his offer. This time he sent a greater company of greater prestige bearing greater wealth. It was truly a royal procession, full of the pomp and circumstance that was certain to stroke the ego of Balaam and display Balak's commitment to honor and reward him for his work. As a matter of fact, the gifts they brought were but a royal down payment; Balak offered to give Balaam anything that was asked of him.

Listen to Balaam's answer, *"Even if Balak were to give me a palace filled with silver and gold, I would be powerless to do anything against the will of the LORD my God."* Now at this point, you are wondering why i am being so harsh on Balaam. This is the right answer, isn't it? Balaam is declaring that he is going to be obedient to what God has told him, right? No, the telling word is the next word – "BUT". Obedience to God will never be followed by the word "BUT". Let me give you an example. Many were walking along the road with Jesus when one turned to Him and said, "I will follow You no matter where you go, BUT first let me return home to bury my father." And another said, "BUT first let me say goodbye to my family." Jesus said, *"Anyone who puts a hand to the plow and then looks back"* – says BUT – *"is not fit for the Kingdom of God"* (Luke 9:57-62). Our obedience must be unfaltering; it must be immediate. Obedience cannot include a "BUT".

Listen to Balaam, instead of standing firm on what God has said, he offers to ask God again, just in the event the offer of greater wealth has caused God to change His mind. The only mind that was being changed was Balaam's, and i'm not sure that this whole process hadn't been a part of his negotiating strategy from the very beginning to get a higher price from Balak. J. Vernon McGee told the story about a preacher *"who came home and told his wife one day, 'Honey, I just had a call from the church over in the next town. Now you know it's a bigger town, richer town, bigger church, more members, and fine folk over there. I've been called to go over there as pastor and I'm going upstairs to pray about it and find out what the Lord's will is for us.' She answered, 'I'll go upstairs to pray with you.' To which the preacher replied, 'Oh no, you stay down here and pack!'"* You see, just like that preacher, Balaam's mind was already made up.

But perhaps you're thinking, "Then why did God tell Balaam to go with the men?" Don't miss this; a lot of us struggle at this very point. We say, "Well, God let me accept the offer, so it must have been His will. Or "God didn't close the door, so it must have been okay with Him." The reality is God will often permit us to do what we have already made up our mind to do. It is not His purposeful will for us, nor is it His perfect will for us, but He will permit us. We may even "pray" about it, like Balaam. But the reality is, we've already made up our mind and we're asking God to bless "our want"; we're not really seeking "His will" (though we will never admit that!).

So let's recap the questions from this passage. Question #1: Are you desperate for God? Are you pursuing His Person and His purpose in this journey with a tenacity that declares a holy desperation for Him? Question #2: Has the Lord clearly led you in a step that He would have you take but you've added a "BUT"? Are you willing to come to a place of abandonment no matter what it costs and remove the "BUT"? Question #3: Are you truly seeking the mind, the heart and the purpose of God? Are you truly seeking Him? Or have you already made up your mind and you just want His permission? (If you are, the reality is that you will do what you want no matter what God says!)

He's leading you on this journey so that you can answer these questions. Perhaps the whole reason you are wandering in the wilderness has to do with your answers. So – what is <u>your</u> answer?

* * *

35

GOD USED A DONKEY

So the next morning Balaam saddled his donkey and started off.... But God was furious that Balaam was going, so he sent the angel of the LORD to stand in the road to block his way. ...Balaam's donkey suddenly saw the angel of the LORD standing in the road with a drawn sword in his hand. The donkey bolted off the road into a field, but Balaam beat it and turned it back onto the road. Then the angel of the LORD stood at a place where the road narrowed between two vineyard walls. When the donkey saw the angel of the LORD standing there, it tried to squeeze by and crushed Balaam's foot against the wall. So Balaam beat the donkey again. Then the angel of the LORD moved farther down the road and stood in a place so narrow that the donkey could not get by at all. This time when the donkey saw the angel, it lay down under Balaam. In a fit of rage Balaam beat it again with his staff. Then the LORD caused the donkey to speak. "What have I done to you that deserves your beating me these three times?" it asked Balaam. "Because you have made me look like a fool!" Balaam shouted. "If I had a sword with me, I would kill you!" "But I am the same donkey you always ride on," the donkey answered. "Have I ever done anything like this before?" "No," he admitted. Then the LORD opened Balaam's eyes, and he saw the angel of the LORD standing in the roadway with a drawn sword in his hand. Balaam fell face down on the ground before him. "...Three times the donkey saw me and shied away; otherwise, I would certainly have killed you by now and spared the donkey." Then Balaam confessed to the angel of the LORD, "I have sinned. I did not realize you were standing in the road to block my way. I will go back home if you are against my going."

Numbers 22:21-34

* * *

That morning Balaam chose to disobey God. Yes, i know that the night before God had told him that he could go. But remember, God's perfect will was that Balaam not go; God's permissive will was allowing Balaam to choose to go his own way. Let there be no confusion, however, the path he had chosen was in disobedience to God. And God confirmed His displeasure with Balaam's disobedience by sending His angel to stand in the road to block his way.

Balaam, who boasted of his ability to hear and see God, couldn't see a thing. Balaam, who was journeying to Moab to profit from speaking for God, didn't have a clue that God's angel stood in his way. Balaam was blinded to the angel's presence. Balaam was blinded by the sin of ambition and his lust for ungodly reward.

But even in his blindness and disobedience, God was gracious to Balaam and placed a fellow traveler on his path - a traveler who could see more clearly. The fellow traveler didn't have much of a pedigree. She wasn't known for her brilliance or her eloquence. She wasn't even known for her ability to hear from God. She was just a simple servant - a beast of burden – one who carried other's burdens. And God had given this traveling companion the assignment of journeying with Balaam that day; as a matter of fact she was charged with Balaam's passage, just as she had, many times before. It is interesting that though Balaam and his donkey were traveling the same path; one saw the angel, the other did not. Both of them were carrying a burden that day; the donkey was carrying a physical burden (Balaam), but even under the weight of her physical burden the donkey could see clearly. Balaam, on the other hand, was traveling under the burden of sin; sin caused by his disobedience. And though a physical burden will not cause spiritual blindness, the burden of sin will. What the donkey could see clearly, Balaam could not see at all. The donkey could see the death and destruction that laid ahead in the path that Balaam was traveling. And Balaam was resolute in his journey. What would the donkey do? The donkey had apparently carried Balaam on many occasions, and she apparently loved her master. In love, she could not allow Balaam to experience the death and destruction that was before him. She realized that because she loved him, she must warn her fellow traveler of the dangers ahead.

First, the donkey attempted to warn Balaam by turning him aside – by pointing him away from the path of destruction. But Balaam's response was typical. You see, those who are resolute in their pursuit of sin and are running headlong into its destruction, will invariably be angry with those who would attempt to dissuade them. They will lash out – physically, verbally, and emotionally. But out of love, the donkey did not allow Balaam's response to keep her from doing what she knew she must do.

Next, the donkey saw that the path ahead was too narrow for them to pass, but she could not dissuade Balaam. She journeyed forward with him knowing that Balaam's foot would be crushed against the wall. The donkey didn't want to see Balaam hurt; she wanted to save him. But she allowed Balaam to move forward in the hopes that the physical pain that would result would seize his attention and save his life. She had to love him enough to not rescue him from a physical consequence of his disobedience. Unfortunately, instead of allowing the pain to turn his attention, it caused Balaam to lash out even more.

Now the donkey had no other recourse. She knew that with each step she took, she was enabling Balaam to move further down the path of destruction. She could no longer enable Balaam in this self-destructive journey. This decision was by far the most difficult for the donkey to make, but she had no other choice. She was a beast of burden, his helper. Her life revolved around carrying her master from one place to another. She had always obeyed her master. Stopping in her tracks went against everything she had ever been taught about being a loyal donkey; but she realized that a donkey that truly loved her master could not carry him into faithless destruction. So she stopped right there. She laid down on the path and would go no further. Balaam did what you would expect; he railed against the donkey.

Then God opened the mouth of the donkey. As she opened her mouth, God used her words to open Balaam's eyes and he saw the angel of the Lord standing in the way. As his eyes were opened he confessed his sin and repented.

Today as you journey in the wilderness, whether you are like Balaam or you are like the donkey, learn from this lesson. The enemy seeks to blind sojourners on the journey. The pathway of sin leads to destruction. If God has opened your eyes to what lays ahead on the path of a fellow traveler, follow the example of this donkey.

• • •

God used the foolish to confound the wise (1 Cor 1:27). God used the faithfulness of that little donkey to open Balaam's eyes. It took courage, it took boldness, but most of all, it took love. The kind of love that Jesus was talking about when He said, *"The greatest love is shown when people lay down their lives for their friends"* (John 15:13).

But one more thing – the same angel that was there to destroy Balaam was there to protect the donkey. The enemy would have us "just go along" for fear of what will happen to us - for fear of rejection or hurt. We must be mindful that the sword of the angel of the Lord not only destroys, it protects.

Stay on the path that God has placed you on and be faithful to His assignment. If God can use a donkey, He can use us – if we will let Him.

* * *

36

AN ATTEMPT TO TEMPT

Then Balaam confessed to the angel of the LORD, "I have sinned...." The angel of the LORD told him, "Go with these men, but you may say only what I tell you to say." ...When King Balak heard that Balaam was on the way, he went out to meet him.... "Did I not send you an urgent invitation? Why didn't you come right away?" Balak asked Balaam. "Didn't you believe me when I said I would reward you richly?" Balaam replied, "I have come, but I have no power to say just anything. I will speak only the messages that God gives me." ...The next morning Balak took Balaam up to Bamoth-baal. From there he could see the people of Israel spread out below him. Balaam said to King Balak, "Build me seven altars here, and prepare seven young bulls and seven rams for a sacrifice." ...Then Balaam said to Balak, "Stand here by your burnt offerings, and I will go to see if the LORD will respond to me...." So Balaam went alone to the top of a hill. ...Then the LORD gave Balaam a message for King Balak and said, "Go back to Balak and tell him what I told you." ...This was the prophecy Balaam delivered: "Balak summoned me to come from Aram; the king of Moab brought me from the eastern hills.' Come,' he said, 'curse Jacob for me! Come and announce Israel's doom.' But how can I curse those whom God has not cursed? How can I condemn those whom the LORD has not condemned? I see them from the cliff tops; I watch them from the hills. I see a people who live by themselves, set apart from other nations. Who can count Jacob's descendants, as numerous as dust? Who can count even a fourth of Israel's people? Let me die like the righteous; let my life end like theirs." Then King Balak demanded of Balaam, "What have you done to me? I brought you to curse my enemies. Instead, you have blessed them!" But Balaam replied, "Can I say anything except what the LORD tells me?"

Numbers 22:34-38, 41; 23:1, 3, 5, 7-12

* * *

Can you imagine Balak's excitement? His plan is coming together! He has contracted the services of Balaam the diviner to curse these dreaded sons of Israel – these distant cousins – this people who he says are a threat to the Moabites. In reality, he sees them as a threat to himself personally – his position as king, his prestige and his possessions – everything that he holds dear and looks to for self-worth. He has just received a report that Balaam is approaching the border of Moab. Balaam, the diviner; Balaam, the one who will curse these Israelites, assuring their defeat and destruction, has finally come. Everything is in place as Balak has planned. Just like a child on Christmas Eve, he can't wait for Balaam to arrive; so Balak travels to the border to meet him. Can you hear the excitement and the impatience in his voice as he asks Balaam, "What took you so long? Didn't you understand that I am going to compensate you well for services well-rendered?"

Balaam's reply, "I can't say just anything; only the messages God gives me", probably meant little to Balak. He probably interpreted that statement has nothing more than this diviner's standard response. Balaam had come to Moab; that could only mean that he had come to curse the Israelites. If you look close, you can almost see Balak winking his eye at Balaam. "Oh, of course you can only say what God tells you to say", as he is thinking, "and what my money has paid you to say."

What Balak didn't understand yet, was that something had happened on the road to Moab. Confronted by the angel of the Lord, Balaam had confessed his sin, repented, and had turned to walk <u>with</u> God. God would now take Balaam's journey that had been meant for evil, transform it and use it to His glory and for His purpose.

Balak determined that they would rest overnight and in the morning he would take Balaam to Bamoth-baal – "the high place of Baal", the false god of the peoples of that region. There they would overlook the people of God camping in the valley below.

As i picture them standing on this high pinnacle that was named to honor a false god, i am reminded of a time over 1400 years later when the god of this world took Jesus to a very high mountain and showed Him all the kingdoms of the world. *"I will give it all to You,' he said, "if You will only kneel down and worship me"* (Matt 4:9). Satan attempted to tempt Jesus with the things of this world; "all" He needed to do was worship the evil one. Jesus responded, *"You must serve the Lord your God; serve only Him"* (Matt 4:10). Balak offered Balaam possessions, position and prestige; "all" he needed to do was curse this people. Just as Satan took Jesus to three different heights to tempt Him, Balak took Balaam to three different overlooks to tempt him (see the second and third locations in Numbers 23:13-30).

The altars were prepared and the sacrifices were offered. Balak either thought that he would go through the motions of at least appearing to seek God's approval of his plan, or perhaps he thought that by going through ritual he could manipulate God or further maneuver this diviner to complete his assignment. But God will not be manipulated and God will not be mocked; and now a repentant Balaam would not be maneuvered.

Those who God had blessed could not be cursed. Balaam spoke the words that God placed in his mouth. Just like Jesus did, he first denounced the wickedness and the deceit of the evil one, then he affirmed God's word and His purpose. The blessings that were spoken over the people of Israel affirmed their possessions, their position and their prestige as the people of God. And Balaam concluded the blessing by saying, *"Let me die like the righteous; let my life end like theirs."* (Unfortunately, as we will see, that was not to be the case.) Balak had attempted to tempt Balaam with the possessions, position and prestige that he had to offer; but as Balaam looked upon God's people, he saw what could not be imitated or counterfeited.

As you journey through the wilderness, the world and the evil one will attempt to tempt you to disobey God with the promises of counterfeits that they have to offer. Remember, only God's word will stand. No one can curse those whom God has not cursed; and no one can curse those whom God has blessed. If you are a child of God, you have been blessed by God. Watch for the attempts to tempt. Walk in His blessings. Stand on His promises. Don't settle for less than His best.

* * *

37

A POWERFUL REBUKE

AND A POTENT REMINDER

"What did the LORD say?" Balak asked eagerly. This was the prophecy Balaam delivered: "Rise up, Balak, and listen! Hear me, son of Zippor. God is not a man, that he should lie. He is not a human, that he should change his mind. Has he ever spoken and failed to act? Has he ever promised and not carried it through?"
Numbers 23:17-19

* * *

Just as these words were a powerful rebuke to a king that sought to manipulate God, they are also a potent reminder to a people that are seeking to follow God. Only Balak heard these words as they were spoken that day, but God had them transcribed and included in His Scripture so that His people – those of yesterday and today and tomorrow – would hear them, hold onto them, and heed them.

"GOD IS NOT A MAN THAT HE SHOULD LIE." That truth stung at the very heart of Balak. Balak's plan to defeat the Israelites was based upon deception, manipulation and compromise. He was confident in his ability to manipulate Balaam through the promise of wealth and prestige to curse a people that God had blessed. Balak believed the adage that too many in our day have also bought into – "the end justifies the means". He was doing all of this to save his kingdom, or so he rationalized it. He was even impressed with his own craftiness. He felt fully justified to manipulate people, to compromise their beliefs and to deceive them through false statements. He had no difficulty attributing words to God that God had not spoken. Though man may "bend" the truth, God will not. Jesus said, *"I am the Truth"* (John 14:6). God is truth; His Word is truth. Henry Blackaby says "You don't know the truth of any situation until you have heard from God." There is no half-truth in what God has said; there is no relative truth in what God has said. There is only full, absolute, uncompromising truth. Truth that is incontrovertible, indisputable and irrefutable.

"GOD IS NOT A HUMAN THAT HE SHOULD CHANGE HIS MIND." Our Lord is the same yesterday, today and forever (Heb 13:8). His Person and His purpose are unchanging. He does not have to reevaluate His instruction based upon new information. God knows the end from the beginning, from before the beginning of time. There is nothing we will encounter that He has not known about from the beginning. There is no "new information" or "change in our situation" that will cause Him to reorder our steps. God will never have to come to us and say, "I'm sorry. I made a mistake. We need to make a change." God is not learning by trial and error. He does not need to experiment. His word does not sway with public opinion. His word does not become outdated by new discoveries. In a world that is in constant change and constant upheaval, God NEVER changes!

GOD WILL NOT PROMISE AND FAIL TO ACT. Our God is not a God of good intentions. He is not a God who intended to do something – who promised to do something – and then was distracted, delayed or detained. How many times have you or i promised to do something and then been too busy or forgotten? Or how many times have we promised something that we couldn't deliver because it was beyond our ability or control? God will NEVER promise anything outside of His ability or control because there is NOTHING outside of His ability or control. That which He promises, He is ABLE to complete. That which He promises, He will move heaven and earth, if need be, to accomplish. That which He promises is as good as begun. Does that mean that what He promises He acts upon in our timeframe and according to our plan, in the way we deem to be best? No, no and no! He will accomplish it according to His timeframe in the way that best accomplishes His purpose and leads to His glory.

GOD WILL NOT PROMISE AND FAIL TO COMPLETE IT. He promises that whatever He begins, He completes (Phil 1:6) and *"He is able to accomplish infinitely more than we would ever dare to ask or hope"* (Eph 3:20). The very fact that you and i are still here walking on this earth is indicative that He is not done working in and through us. Lest this come as a giant shock – HE IS THE POTTER, we are just the clay; HE IS THE CREATOR, we are His creation. We have been created in His image for His purpose. Why do we keep trying to turn that around – trying to recreate Him into the image we think He should be like, in order to accomplish our selfish and self-centered purpose?

God promised us a Savior. And two thousand years ago, He so loved the world that He sent His only Son (John 3:16). And this same Jesus has promised to come again (John 14:3). It may or may not be in my lifetime or in yours, but He will complete His promise, and in the meantime He is working in and through our lives to continue the fulfillment of His purpose.

Though this message was spoken to Balak on the mountaintop, it was just as true for the Israelites in the valley. And it is just as true for you and me as we continue our journey through the wilderness. Do you remember the promise God gave you when the journey began? Well then heed His potent reminder: God does not lie! He does not change His mind! He will not fail to act! And He will finish what He has started!

* * *

38

I CAN SEE CLEARLY NOW

Then Balak said to Balaam, "If you aren't going to curse them, at least don't bless them!" But Balaam replied, "Didn't I tell you that I must do whatever the LORD tells me?" ...Then the Spirit of God came upon him, and this is the prophecy he delivered: "This is the prophecy of Balaam son of Beor, the prophecy of the man whose eyes see clearly, who hears the words of God, who sees a vision from the Almighty, who falls down with eyes wide open: ...Blessed is everyone who blesses you, O Israel, and cursed is everyone who curses you."
Numbers 23:25-26; 24:2-4, 9

* * *

In the early 1970's a song was released entitled *"I Can See Clearly Now"*. A portion of the lyrics of the first verse go like this: *"I can see clearly now, the rain is gone.... Gone are the dark clouds that had me blind. It's gonna be a bright (bright), bright (bright), sun shiny day."* When the Spirit of God came upon Balaam, he could see clearly now, the rain and the clouds that had blinded him were gone; and he could see as under the bright noonday sun. Light had dawned in the darkness and the darkness had been obliterated by the noonday sun. That is what light does, it eradicates darkness. It is interesting to note that no amount of darkness can dispel the light, but even a little bit of light will disperse the darkness.

Balak thought he could beat off the light of God with darkness. He thought he could overshadow the blessings of God with cursings. That is why he had contracted Balaam's services for hire. That is why he had taken Balaam to three different mountaintops – to do just that – to curse the people of Israel from the darkness. And that makes perfect sense – when you live in the darkness. Because in the darkness you are blinded from seeing anything clearly. You can't see the path ahead; you are feeling your way around hoping that you are going the right way. There is an expression "blind luck" that is used by people who live their lives in darkness. It assumes that the only way you can experience blessings in the journey is if you happen to stumble over them or they stumble over you. Apart from that chance happening, everyone is destined to wander and suffer in the darkness. Since Balak was wandering in the darkness, he wanted the Israelites to be cursed to wander in the darkness like him. And Balaam had set out on his journey the same way, until he confessed his sin and turned from his sin. Then the Holy Spirit came upon him.

i think a lot of us are wandering in the wilderness when God intends for us to be in the Promised Land – and it is because of our blindness. We're feeling our way around, stumbling all over ourselves, unable to discern the path ahead. Well, i've got good news – if you will confess your sin and turn from it, you can be assured that the Holy Spirit will come upon you, just as He did Balaam. And when the Holy Spirit comes upon you, "it's gonna be a bright, bright, sun shiny day." AND WHEN THAT HAPPENS:

Just like Balaam, YOU WILL SEE CLEARLY. Because God will enable you to see from His perspective. There are no obstacles that God can't see over, around or past. He clearly sees the other side. Only He has perfect vision, and He will enable you to see perfectly. Now there may be times in your journey that He delays in allowing you to see clearly because you aren't yet prepared to see what He is going to show you. Take heart, He is preparing you to see, and in His time YOU WILL SEE CLEARLY.

Just like Balaam, YOU WILL HEAR THE WORDS OF GOD. Apart from the Spirit of God giving us understanding, in our flesh we are deaf to the word of God. Paraphrasing what Paul said, "To the man of flesh, it is foolishness" (1 Cor 2:14). But when His Spirit comes upon us, our ears are unstopped to hear and our hearts are unstopped to receive His Word. And His Word becomes *"a lamp to my feet, and a light to my path"* (Psa 119:105). Henry Blackaby says, "We have not heard the truth of any situation, until we have heard from God." There is no truth apart from God's truth; there is no true direction apart from God's direction. And in the proper time, you will hear that "word aptly spoken" (Prov 25:11 NIV); YOU WILL HEAR THE WORDS OF GOD.

. . .

Just like Balaam, YOU WILL SEE THE VISION OF WHAT GOD HAS SET BEFORE YOU. Jesus told the apostles, "But when the Holy Spirit has come upon you, you will receive power…" (Acts 1:8). From the day of Jesus' arrest until the Day of Pentecost, the apostles scattered and hid and waited, but that day when the Holy Spirit filled them with His presence not only was that room shaken, so were their lives. They were never again the same. They never saw things the same again. God had given them a vision – His vision – for reaching the world. Jesus had given them His commission before He ascended into heaven, but the apostles didn't catch the vision until the Holy Spirit came upon them. God sent His Holy Spirit that we might be equipped and empowered for the accomplishment of His vision – not ours. As in all things, God will choose the timing; but be confident of this – if the Spirit of God has come upon you, YOU WILL SEE THE VISION OF WHAT GOD HAS SET BEFORE YOU.

And lastly, just like Balaam, YOU WILL FALL DOWN AND WORSHIP GOD WITH EYES WIDE OPEN. Once God enables us to see clearly, in fact He will enable us to see Him more clearly; and once that happens, our response will be to worship Him. Not with eyes closed, but with eyes wide open; because once He opens our eyes, and our eyes are truly opened we will never want them to be closed again. We will desire to see more and more of Him; to know Him, to know Him more, and to know Him more intimately. Yes, when the Spirit of God has come upon you, YOU WILL FALL DOWN AND WORSHIP GOD WITH EYES WIDE OPEN.

Balaam went on to speak God's blessing over the people of Israel. But do you know who i believe received the greater blessing that day? i believe it was Balaam – because the Holy Spirit came upon him! And i believe that there is no greater blessing that God gives His children apart from salvation than the indwelling presence of His Holy Spirit.

So if you're still wandering in the wilderness, make sure that you have confessed your sin and turned from it. If you have, you are assured of the indwelling presence of the Holy Spirit – you have received God's blessing – all the rest will come to pass in His timing. He has already enabled you to say with confidence, "I CAN SEE CLEARLY NOW."

* * *

39

WHICH REWARD – THE CHOICE IS OURS!

King Balak flew into a rage against Balaam. He angrily clapped his hands and shouted, "I called you to curse my enemies! Instead, you have blessed them three times. Now get out of here! Go back home! I had planned to reward you richly, but the LORD has kept you from your reward." Balaam told Balak, "...I told you that I could say only what the LORD says! Now I am returning to my own people. But first let me tell you what the Israelites will do to your people in the future." This is the prophecy Balaam delivered: "...A star will rise from Jacob; a scepter will emerge from Israel. It will crush the foreheads of Moab's people, cracking the skulls of the people of Sheth."

Numbers 24:10-17

The other day as i was subscribing to a new phone service, i was told that i was eligible to receive a reward for becoming a new customer. i could choose to receive frequent flyer miles with an airline of my choice, or i could choose to receive reward points with the hotel chain of my choice. My response was to say that i would like both. The customer service representative laughed and said, "Wouldn't we all! But you can only have one; you must choose which one you will receive."

Listen to the words of Balak, "I had planned to reward you richly, but the LORD has kept you from your reward." As we have already seen, Balak's promised reward consisted of the best he had to offer – wealth, position and fame. All Balaam had to do to receive his reward was participate in Balak's deception. All he had to do was attribute to God words that He never said. All Balaam had to do was utter a curse where God had uttered a blessing. Who would know? It wouldn't require a lot of work or much effort. All he had to do was curse this people and the reward was his. All Balaam had to do was disobey God!

Whereas if Balaam obeyed God and turned from his sin, God's Spirit would come upon him. Filled with God's Spirit, Balaam could be assured that he would see clearly, he would hear God's voice, and he would know God's revealed will. He would walk in relationship and in fellowship with God. He would experience the intimacy of a faithful walk with the Lord God Jehovah. All Balaam had to do was obey God!

Rewards are no better and no more reliable than the one who offers them. Balak's rewards were offered at his whim and at his pleasure. Balak's promises could be broken, his mind might change or his plan from the outset may have been to deceive Balaam. Balak's rewards were at best momentary; position and prestige are fleeting, and possessions can be taken from us or corrupted or destroyed. No, as attractive as Balak's rewards might be, even if they were given, they would not last.

On the other hand, the rewards of obedience to God were assured by the word of God, the character of God and the power of God. There would never be a concern that He didn't mean what He said or that He had changed His mind. That which God gives cannot be taken away by another; and that which God gives endures forever.

Balak was right about one thing though: you cannot receive the rewards for deceit and disobedience AND the rewards for faithful obedience. They are mutually exclusive. You can't "have the best of both worlds". There is no such thing as the best of both worlds. Darkness and light cannot dwell together. James writes that the double-minded man is unstable in all his ways (Jas 1:8). Balaam's obedience to God did keep him from receiving Balak's reward. You will receive one at the cost of the other. And that is a choice that we must make. It is the choice that has existed since time began in the Garden of Eden. Adam and Eve had to decide which reward they would choose – the promises of Satan or the promises of God. They did not choose well; and their choice led to the choice that was set before Balaam. It was their choice that has led to the choice that is set before you and me.

. . .

But as we close out the account of Balak and Balaam, we should see one more thing. Balak thought that it was by his power that one was exalted and another was put down. He thought he could decide who would be cursed and who would be blessed. Many of us today make that same mistake. From the days of the early patriarchs we read:

> *"He sets on high those who are lowly,*
> *And those who mourn are lifted to safety.*
> *He frustrates the devices of the crafty,*
> *So that their hands cannot carry out their plans.*
> *He catches the wise in their own craftiness,*
> *And the counsel of the cunning comes quickly upon them."*

(Job 5:11-13 NKJ)

It is God who exalts; and it is God who puts down. Those who would curse those who God blesses will themselves be cursed. Those who would bless those who God blesses will themselves be blessed.

As we journey in the wilderness, we too have been given the opportunity to choose our reward. Will we choose the rewards that this world has to offer, or the rewards of our Lord God Jehovah? We can't have them both; we must decide. Choose well; your choice will not only affect the remainder of your journey, it will affect those who come after you as well.

* * *

40

ONE STEP TO STUPID

Then Balaam and Balak returned to their homes. While the Israelites were camped at Acacia, some of the men defiled themselves by sleeping with the local Moabite women. These women invited them to attend sacrifices to their gods, and soon the Israelites were feasting with them and worshiping the gods of Moab. Before long Israel was joining in the worship of Baal of Peor, causing the LORD's anger to blaze against his people.
Numbers 24:25; 25:1-3

* * *

For the past few chapters, we have seen Balaam make the right choices. We have seen him used by God to bless His people. But as we bring our attention back to the Israelite camp, we see the Israelite men pursuing the Moabite women, and in the process, worshipping the Moabite gods. And God's anger begins "to blaze against His people."

Here, all this time Balak, king of the Moabites, has been attempting to have God's curse pronounced over the Israelites through the prophet Balaam; but now through their own actions the Israelites draw God's anger upon themselves. Perhaps all Balak needed to have done was just wait and allow the Israelites to curse themselves through their own disobedience. Unfortunately that is a story we have seen replayed time and again by this people as they have journeyed through the wilderness; a recurring pattern of disobedience. But the fact of the matter is, they got some help this time. There was one who knew how easily this people could be tempted to disobey God. This same one knew that this people were the people of God. He knew that no one could curse those whom God had blessed; and no one could defeat the people whom God protected – EXCEPT the people themselves. Only the Israelites through their own disobedience could bring God's curses upon themselves; only their disobedience could cause them to experience defeat and destruction at the hand of God. One man saw how easily this people could be tempted to disobey God. He saw how easily this people could be led to take that one step from godliness into sin. He knew that this people were at a place that, as my friend and former pastor Dr. Keith Thomas said, "was only one step to stupid".

Balaam was not tempted by the Moabite women; he was tempted by wealth. As much as his heart had been changed on the back of that donkey that day, there was apparently a stronghold in Balak's life that he didn't bring under the lordship of God. He had lived his life to that point "divining for dollars". He had developed quite a reputation, and apparently amassed a fair fortune in the process. But when it comes to money, too often, it is never enough. Balak was offering Balaam a pretty good "chunk of change". Balaam knew that he could not do what Balak asked; he could not curse these Israelites. But it would appear that Balaam never stopped trying to come up with a way to obey God and still line his pockets. At some point before "Balaam and Balak returned to their homes", Balaam came up with a way that Balak could get what he wanted (a way to curse the Israelites), and Balaam could get what he wanted (the cash). Yes, Balaam was the author of the script to tempt the Israelites. He devised the plan and gave it to Balak to execute.

The most direct word of witness that we are given in Scripture that Balaam was the culprit comes from God Himself. Jesus said, "*Balaam … showed Balak how to trip up the people of Israel. He taught them to worship idols by eating food offered to idols and by committing sexual sin*" (Rev 2:14). Apart from this word of witness, we might have missed that Balaam was the transgressor. His sin may have remained covered from our view, but God uncovers it as a reminder to us that we cannot cover our sin. We cannot sin outside of God's view and He will not allow our sin to remain covered.

Andrew Fausset writes, "Trying to combine prophecy and soothsaying, the service of God and the wages of iniquity, Balaam made the choice that ruined him forever! He wanted to do opposite things at once, to curse and to bless (James 3:9-10), to earn at once the wages of righteousness and unrighteousness, if possible not to offend God, yet not to lose Balak's reward." Balaam's plan led him right back down the slippery slope of sin. He who had honored God now dishonored Him by laying a plan that caused God's people to stumble. In Chapter 31 we see God's punishment for his disobedience. He, who had been blessed mightily by God, now would experience the wrath of God. He who stood on the mount and was used by God to bless His people would now die in the valley by the sword of God's judgment. And the journey was one step - one step of disobedience – one step to stupid.

Balaam needed to heed the word that Paul later wrote to his son in the ministry, Timothy: *"For the love of money is at the root of all kinds of evil. And some people, craving money, have wandered from the faith and pierced themselves with many sorrows. But you, Timothy, belong to God; so run from all these evil things, and follow what is right and good. Pursue a godly life, along with faith, love, perseverance, and gentleness. ...Obey His commands with all purity. Then no one can find fault with you from now until our Lord Jesus Christ returns"* (1 Tim 6:10-11, 14).

God has called you; he has set you apart unto Himself and has led you on this journey. As you continue step by step, do so with the awareness that it is only one step to stupid for each and every one of us. Whenever you are trying to figure out how to go your own way and still be obedient to God – you're taking that step to stupid. Whenever you find yourself rationalizing disobedience – you're taking that step to stupid. Whenever you attempt to cover your sin – you're taking that step to stupid. Heed the word and the warning that God gave through the life of Balaam, as well as His prophet Nahum, *"I will lift your skirts so all the earth will see your nakedness and shame. I will cover you with filth and show the world how vile you really are"* (Nah 3:5-6). Remember, there is no one who can curse those whom God has blessed; and no one who can defeat the people whom God protects – EXCEPT we ourselves. Don't take that step!

* * *

41

KEEP YOURSELF PURE

While the Israelites were camped at Acacia, some of the men defiled themselves by sleeping with the local Moabite women. These women invited them to attend sacrifices to their gods, and soon the Israelites were feasting with them and worshiping the gods of Moab. Before long Israel was joining in the worship of Baal of Peor, causing the LORD's anger to blaze against his people. The LORD issued the following command to Moses: "Seize all the ringleaders and execute them before the LORD in broad daylight, so his fierce anger will turn away from the people of Israel." So Moses ordered Israel's judges to execute everyone who had joined in worshiping Baal of Peor. Just then one of the Israelite men brought a Midianite woman into the camp, right before the eyes of Moses and all the people, as they were weeping at the entrance of the Tabernacle. When Phinehas son of Eleazar and grandson of Aaron the priest saw this, he jumped up and left the assembly. Then he took a spear and rushed after the man into his tent. Phinehas thrust the spear all the way through the man's body and into the woman's stomach. So the plague against the Israelites was stopped, but not before 24,000 people had died. ...The Israelite man killed with the Midianite woman was named Zimri son of Salu, the leader of a family from the tribe of Simeon. The woman's name was Cozbi; she was the daughter of Zur, the leader of a Midianite clan. Then the LORD said to Moses, "Attack the Midianites and destroy them, because they assaulted you with deceit by tricking you into worshiping Baal of Peor, and because of Cozbi, the daughter of a Midianite leader, who was killed on the day of the plague at Peor."

Numbers 25:1-9, 14-18

* * *

You will recall that the Moabites and the Midianites had formed an alliance; its purpose being to destroy the Israelites. When Balak's plan to destroy them through the curse of Balaam failed, they turned to Balaam's recommended strategy to defeat them through sexual temptation. The strategy was to lure the Israelite men into worshipping their pagan gods through the enticement of sexual favor. And unfortunately, this strategy worked; some of the men began to join in on the worship of Baal. We don't know all of their names, but we do know two.

Zimri, whose name means "wild goat", was a prince of the tribe of Simeon, the second son of Jacob by Leah. It was Simeon who, together with his younger brother Levi, had defended the honor of their sister Dinah when she was raped and defiled by Shechem the Hivite (Gen 34). The Hivites were willing to circumcise themselves for the lust of the Israelite women. And Simeon and Levi slaughtered every man in Schechem's village while they were recovering from their circumcision. Their merciless retribution on the Hivites had even caused Jacob to declare that Simeon had made the Israelites despicable in the eyes of the people in and around the Promised Land. Though the sons of Simeon were unswerving in the defense of the sexual purity of Simeonite women, they apparently did not harbor that same conviction about themselves. And now the same sin of succumbing to sexual temptation and lust for which they had punished the inhabitants of Canaan, was to be their downfall here at Acacia.

Cozbi, whose name means "deceitful", was a princess of the tribe of Midian. She and the other young women of her tribe had been commanded by the kings of Midian to entice and seduce the men of Israel and to lead them to attend their pagan worship feasts.

The Lord had just instructed Moses to execute the men of Israel that had led in this abomination. And in the middle of this judgment, into the camp walks Prince "Wild Goat" leading Princess "Deceitful". In the midst of their sin, Zimri and Cozbi were oblivious to what was going on in the camp. They were blinded to the judgment that was coming their way. Isn't that what sin does? It blinds us and turns our attention from where it should be to where it should not be. Sin had led Zimri, and all the other men, to turn their eyes from the one true God, the God of Abraham, Isaac and Jacob, to the false gods of the Moabites and Midianites. That truth is the same today as well. The effect of sin is that it turns our eyes and our hearts away from God to the false gods of this world, and we too become blind and oblivious to the truth.

The penalty for the sin of Zimri and Cozbi was physical death. Now before you rush to ask why God punished them so severely, remember God's purpose for His people. God had set them apart for one purpose – to be His people through whom He would make His Name known for His glory. There was no room in His purpose for the worship of other gods. This people had been set apart by Him for His purpose. As these men turned and worshipped the false god of Baal they dishonored the Lord God Jehovah, bringing derision on His Name. God's purpose required that they remain pure and cleansed vessels – vessels of honor. His judgment was swift to protect the testimony of His people.

Perhaps you are asking, why didn't God kill the Midianites and spare the Israelites? After all, the Midianites had tempted and tricked the Israelites. Well, God did punish the Midianites, as we will see in Numbers 31; but the Israelites were no less accountable for their response to that temptation. Bear in mind that our response to temptation merely reveals what is in our heart. The temptation did not cause the Israelites to sin; sin was how they chose to respond to the temptation.

Heed this lesson. God has set you apart for one purpose – to be His people through whom He makes His Name known for His glory. That's why we are here. That is why Paul wrote to Timothy, "*If you keep yourself pure, you will be a utensil God can use for his purpose. Your life will be clean, and you will be ready for the Master to use you for every good work*" (2 Tim 2:21). But if we don't keep ourselves pure, we will not be utensils that He can use. i am mindful that in our home, when it is time to clean out the drawers in our kitchen, we don't hold onto the utensils that we can no longer use. We get rid of them to make room for those we can use; or if they have become contaminated in some way, so that they do not contaminate the others. God does the same thing!

Keep yourself pure, cleansed and ready for the Master.

* * *

42

A PASSIONATE PURSUIT OF GOD

Just then one of the Israelite men brought a Midianite woman into the camp, right before the eyes of Moses and all the people, as they were weeping at the entrance of the Tabernacle. When Phinehas son of Eleazar and grandson of Aaron the priest saw this, he jumped up and left the assembly. Then he took a spear and rushed after the man into his tent. Phinehas thrust the spear all the way through the man's body and into the woman's stomach. So the plague against the Israelites was stopped, but not before 24,000 people had died. Then the LORD said to Moses, "Phinehas son of Eleazar and grandson of Aaron the priest has turned my anger away from the Israelites by displaying passionate zeal among them on my behalf. So I have stopped destroying all Israel as I had intended to do in my anger. So tell him that I am making my special covenant of peace with him. In this covenant, he and his descendants will be priests for all time, because he was zealous for his God and made atonement for the people of Israel."

Numbers 25:6-13

* * *

You will recall that the Israelites had come under the judgment of God because of their sinful pursuit of the women and false gods of Moab and Midian. God had issued the command, and Moses had so ordered *"Israel's judges to execute everyone who had joined in worshipping Baal"* (Num 25:5). As those executions were underway, Zimri led the Midianite woman into the camp, not only in disobedience to God, but also in defiance of God. All of the people saw what was happening, but only one jumped up; and Phinehas then thrust his spear into Zimri and the woman.

. . .

Before we go any further, we need to be clear that Phinehas was functioning under the command of God and the orders of Moses. He was under Divine authority as well as civil authority. Phinehas, as the heir apparent to the High Priest, would have been one of the judges so directed by Moses. As we look at the zeal that Phinehas displayed, we must first see that it was zeal submitted to authority. Without submission to authority, zeal will become license for rebellion; ultimately even rebellion against the very "thing" or 'person" for which we are zealous. Zimri and Cozbi had come under the judgment of God, not under the judgment of Phinehas. There was no question as to under whose authority Phinehas was acting.

God affirmed Phinehas' action in two ways. First, because of Phinehas' action God stopped the plaque. 24,000 people had died; but there is no telling how many more would have died if Phinehas had not immediately obeyed. Scripture clearly ties the conclusion of this plague to his obedience. Secondly, because of Phinehas' action God honored him. God made a covenant with Phinehas that he and his descendants would serve Him as priests for all time.

So what is the action that Phinehas displayed that we need to learn from? And no, the answer is not how to thrust a spear! God honored him because *"he was zealous for his God and made atonement for the people."* How did he make atonement for the people? By being obedient to God.

Phinehas *"was zealous for his God."* To be zealous (according to Webster's Revised Unabridged Dictionary © 1998) is to be "filled with or characterized by" a passionate, intense pursuit "in behalf of something" or someone. Phinehas was passionate in his pursuit of God, for God and with God. It was this character that defined him. Others before and since have been obedient, but Phinehas was zealous in his obedience. The psalmist wrote, *"Then Phinehas stood up and intervened, and the plague was stopped. And that was accounted to him for righteousness to all generations forevermore"* (Ps 106:30-31 NKJ). In Scripture, only one other person is commemorated in this manner; and that is Abraham, who was regarded as a righteous man because of his belief in God (Gen 15:6 and Rom 4:3).

The passionate pursuit that Phinehas displayed originated from God. A. W. Tozer wrote in *"The Pursuit of God"*, *"We pursue God because, and only because, He has first put an urge within us that spurs us to the pursuit. The impulse to pursue God originates with God, but the outworking of that impulse is our following hard after Him; and all the time we are pursuing Him we are already in His hand."* That kind of zeal begins and ends in God and can find no satisfaction apart from God. It is a zeal that having begun with God is unextinguishable, since it ends in God is unending, and since it flows out of our fellowship with God is unlimited.

Our God is a God of passion. The Father demonstrated His passion for us through the ultimate sacrifice of His Son, and the Son demonstrated His passion for the Father through His obedience, even unto the cross. He is prepared to instill in our hearts that same passion through the presence of His Spirit.

We live in a world today that is passionate in its pursuits of the things of this world; even we, as followers of Christ, have become passionate in those pursuits. But we have been created and redeemed for only one purpose - to passionately pursue God. When will our zealousness for God exceed our zealousness for the things of this world? Again, Phinehas didn't just obey; he was zealous in his obedience because he was zealous for his God.

O LORD, we who travel on this journey, beseech You to empty us of any zeal we have for anything or anyone other than You; and fill us with a zeal <u>of</u> You, <u>for</u> You and <u>with</u> You. Give us a passionate pursuit for You that is conspicuous to and contagious by the watching world that surrounds us.

* * *

43

THE TIME HAS COME

They were counted by families--all the men of Israel who were twenty years old or older and able to go to war. The total number was 603,550. ...So the total number of Israelite men counted in the census numbered 601,730. Then the LORD said to Moses, "Divide the land among the tribes in proportion to their populations, as indicated by the census." ...So these are the census figures of the people of Israel as prepared by Moses and Eleazar the priest on the plains of Moab beside the Jordan River, across from Jericho. Not one person that Moses and Aaron counted in this census had been among those counted in the previous census taken in the wilderness of Sinai. For the LORD had said of them, "They will all die in the wilderness." The only exceptions were Caleb son of Jephunneh and Joshua son of Nun.

Numbers 1:45-46; 26:51-53, 63-65

* * *

God said to Moses, "Divide the land... in proportion to their population." They had not yet crossed into the Promised Land to occupy it. They had not yet conquered those who currently inhabited the land. With the exception of Caleb and Joshua, none of them had seen the land. And yet, God said, "Divide it. It is yours." God did not say, "Once you have crossed over the Jordan, and after you have defeated the Canaanites and established the land to be yours, then divide it." He was saying, "Divide it now. It is yours already."

Though the people had not stepped foot in the land, it was already their possession. It didn't belong to the Canaanites, Hittites, Perizzites, Hivites or Jebusites; it belonged to God and He had determined that His people would dwell there. When did it become the possession of the people? At the moment that God determined that it would be their possession; and God knew it and determined it before the beginning of time. Others had dwelt there; others had inhabited the land, but no one, other than the people of God, could possess the land. The census was God's listing of His heirs to the land.

Out of the 603,550 men who were counted in the first census in the wilderness of Sinai, 603,548 had died. In the thirty-eight plus years since the rebellion at Kadesh, all but three, including Moses, had died. As a matter of fact, the new census was taken to confirm that none of the original census other than these three was still alive. It signaled that the time had come. Moses was now 120 years old, Joshua was 95, Caleb was 78 and everyone else was 58 years old or younger. Imagine how all of the tribe looked at these three old men of faith. With the exception of Joshua and Caleb, Moses was now better than twice as old as the oldest man among the people. Again with the exception of these three old men, the average age of the tribe was 29; that means probably two-thirds of these people were born in the wilderness. Only one third had any firsthand memory of Egypt, and for most of them the memories were faint. Two-thirds had never experienced an Egyptian whip on their back. Two-thirds couldn't remember a day without manna to eat. Two-thirds couldn't remember a day without a pillar of cloud going before them or dwelling in their midst. Two-thirds had been taught the commandments of God from birth. These were God's people. They had learned to follow God and to depend on God. Were they a perfect people? By no means. Were there people in their midst that continued to seek to go their own way? Unfortunately yes. But these were a people who God had prepared in the wilderness to enter into His land and possess His land.

Though the land was already their possession, it would require work to possess it. It would require courage, strength and stamina. It would require faithful obedience that trusted God's Person, purpose and power. It would require obedience to His Word, even when His Word did not make sense to their human minds.

Those that had tried to reason it out had been buried in the wilderness, at the rate of approximately fifty men per day. They had tried to reason it out but it didn't compute with their human reasoning, so they rebelled against

God. Those daily funeral services were a reminder to the people of this new census of the disobedience of their fathers and the faithfulness of their God. You experience that same message fifty times a day, every day, for thirty-eight years and it starts to sink in. And finally these people were ready.

What is it going to take for you to be ready to enter into your Promised Land? How long do you need to stay in the wilderness before you are ready to move on? Take heart in knowing that the land God has promised you is already your possession. And when you are ready, He will lead you into the land to possess that which is already your possession. But it will be God Who determines when you are ready – not you. When He determines you're ready, He will call for an accounting – a census – a declaration of His heirs, positioned and postured to receive their inheritance; a people prepared to bring glory to God. Yes, He will declare that the time has come.

* * *

44

THE DAUGHTERS OF ZELOPHEHAD

One day a petition was presented by the daughters of Zelophehad--Mahlah, Noah, Hoglah, Milcah, and Tirzah. Their father, Zelophehad, was the son of Hepher, son of Gilead, son of Makir, son of Manasseh, son of Joseph. These women went and stood before Moses, Eleazar the priest, the tribal leaders, and the entire community at the entrance of the Tabernacle. "Our father died in the wilderness without leaving any sons," they said. "But he was not among Korah's followers, who rebelled against the LORD. He died because of his own sin. Why should the name of our father disappear just because he had no sons? Give us property along with the rest of our relatives." So Moses brought their case before the LORD. And the LORD replied to Moses, "The daughters of Zelophehad are right. You must give them an inheritance of land along with their father's relatives. Assign them the property that would have been given to their father. Moreover announce this to the people of Israel: 'If a man dies and has no sons, then give his inheritance to his daughters. And if he has no daughters, turn his inheritance over to his brothers. If he has no brothers, give his inheritance to his father's brothers. But if his father has no brothers, pass on his inheritance to the nearest relative in his clan. The Israelites must observe this as a general legal requirement, just as the LORD commanded Moses.'"

Numbers 27:1-11

* * *

The daughters of Zelophehad were the only living descendants of the subclan of the Hepherites of the tribe of Manasseh. The fact that there were no male heirs in this subclan was so unusual and unique that mention was made of it in the accounting of the census in Numbers 26:33.

You will recall that the census had been taken of the men of Israel at the Lord's command for the purpose of apportioning the Promised Land. Though the daughters of Zelophehad were mentioned in the census, they were to receive no apportionment; the land was to be divided among the 601,730 men.

Among this people of two million plus, this situation is so unique that it again comes up in Numbers 36. As a result of the unusual condition of these women, the Lord further clarifies that the apportioned land of the Promised Land may not pass from one tribe to another; it must stay within that tribe (Num 36:9).

Coming back to this passage, the daughters of Zelophehad realized that they were to have no share in the blessings of the Promised Land. They knew that due to the condition under which they were born, they had no right, title or inheritance in the promise. They had no birthright, and therefore they would receive no portion. So they did the only thing they could do; they called upon the Lord God Jehovah through Moses and the elders. They called upon the One who is the Father of the fatherless and the Father of the faithful.

The daughters knew that their earthly father's name, Zelophehad, meant "protection against fear". He raised them to know that their true and sure protection against fear was the Lord God Jehovah, and that God is the Father of the fatherless. He defends the poor and the orphaned, He upholds the rights of the oppressed and the destitute, and He rescues the poor and the helpless (Psa 82:3-4). There was only One to whom they could truly turn; only He would meet them at the point of their need with grace and compassion. It is a credit to Moses here that he did not attempt to resolve this on his own. God had set forth the plan of apportionment. Moses could not presume to alter the direction given by God; only God could make provision for these daughters.

But also see the faith that these daughters demonstrated. At this point the land was still unconquered and untouched by the Israelites. The land was still inhabited by the giants and fortresses that had kept their fathers from following the Lord into the land. And yet these daughters petitioned God for their just share of the land as if the people already had possession. It has been said that faith "is believing that it is so, even when it isn't so, in order for it to be so, because God said it's so." There was no question in the mind of these daughters that God had given this land to His children, and by faith they sought their portion of His promise.

As we journey in the wilderness, there is much to be gained by following the example of these daughters of Zelophehad. We can approach our Lord with the same courage, confidence and boldness. Though sin has made us a people who are separated from our Heavenly Father, He by His grace, through His Son, has made a way that we can come to Him – that we can experience His grace, His mercy and His love as the Father of the fatherless. And He has given us His promise that assures us of a future and a hope in Him – our apportionment – if we will but by faith receive it. Yes, He is the Father of the fatherless and the Father of the faithful. Receive your apportionment today. He has already set it apart for you. He is just waiting for you to ask for it.

* * *

45

A SELFLESS SERVANT STEPS ASIDE

Then Moses said to the LORD, "O LORD, the God of the spirits of all living things, please appoint a new leader for the community. Give them someone who will lead them into battle, so the people of the LORD will not be like sheep without a shepherd." The LORD replied, "Take Joshua son of Nun, who has the Spirit in him, and lay your hands on him. Present him to Eleazar the priest before the whole community, and publicly commission him with the responsibility of leading the people. Transfer your authority to him so the whole community of Israel will obey him." …So Moses did as the LORD commanded and presented Joshua to Eleazar the priest and the whole community. Moses laid his hands on him and commissioned him to his responsibilities, just as the LORD had commanded through Moses.

Numbers 27:15-20, 22-23

* * *

God had told Moses at the waters of Meribah that he would not lead the people into the Promised Land. Now as the time approached, God prompted Moses to begin to make preparation for the people to enter into the land without him. One of those preparations was the selection of an undershepherd to lead the people. As we come to the beginning of this leadership transition, i want us to look at some of the traits that are evident in Moses' character.

We have already seen the passage of responsibility as high priest from Aaron to his son Eleazar; and we have already seen the selection of

Phinehas to follow his father Eleazar when the time should come. Aaron's descendants had been chosen by God to serve Him in perpetuity as priests, and the balance of the tribe of Levi were to assist Aaron and his descendants in that task. Now we recall that Aaron was Moses' brother. That means that Moses' children and their descendants were to serve in a subordinate role to Aaron's descendants - Aaron, the one who had given in to the pressure from the people at Sinai and crafted the golden calf; Aaron, the one who had on more than one occasion taken the "safe" posture of going along with the crowd. His descendants would for perpetuity be in a position of authority over the descendants of Moses. And speaking of the descendants of Moses, what had happened to them? Moses' wife Zipporah and their two sons, Gershom and Eliezer had been reunited at Sinai (Ex 18:5). The last mention that is made of Zipporah is when Miriam and Aaron jealously criticized Moses at Hazeroth (Num 12:1). Now remember, Moses is 120 years old. The probability is that Zipporah and even possibly their two sons were buried in the wilderness. Gershom and Eliezer and now their children were a part of the Kohathite clan that cared for the utensils and furnishings used in the sanctuary of the tabernacle. There is no indication that any of Moses' descendants are ever placed in a position of leadership.

In those times, as in ours, it was not uncommon for positions of authority and privilege to pass within a family from one generation to the next. It is interesting to note that Moses apparently made no effort to do so. Moses demonstrated a humility and a self-denial that is rarely seen, even in Scripture. It is the kind of humility that Paul spoke of regarding Jesus, when he says that He *"made Himself of no reputation, taking the form of a bondservant, and coming in the likeness of men"* (Phil 2:7 NKJ). Moses was not about building a kingdom; he was about serving the Lord God Jehovah. Moses' actions make it obvious that **he was not acting from himself, because he did not act for himself.**

Moses was a man who sought the counsel of God and obeyed the command of God. It is indicative of the same passion exhibited by our Lord Jesus Christ to *"not seek My own will but the will of the Father who sent Me"* (John 5:30 NKJ). It is ironic that the very reason that he was not leading the people into the Promised Land was because of a rare instance of disobedience, when at Meribah he disregarded the counsel and the command of God. But i also believe that it was because Moses had finished the race; he had completed the assignment that God had for him, and now, God was allowing him to enter into his reward and his rest. But we'll explore that further a little later on.

. . .

But see how God led His servant Moses to appoint Joshua to continue in the work. First, he trained Joshua. For most, if not all, of their forty years in the wilderness, Joshua had served as Moses' understudy. Moses had kept him at his side so that he could watch and observe and learn. Second, he ordained Joshua. He set him apart by the laying on of hands and blessed him. Third, he presented Joshua. He publicly acknowledged Joshua's elevation to this position of authority. He made sure that all of the people knew. Fourth, he commissioned Joshua. He publicly charged him with the responsibility of leading the people. Last, he authorized Joshua. He honored him by transferring authority to him. In essence, Moses was stepping out of the "limelight" so that it would shine on Joshua.

That whole process is the same one that Jesus used in appointing His disciples. Jesus trained them, He set them apart, He presented them, He charged them with His commission, and He authorized them as He empowered them through His Holy Spirit. It is the same process that Jesus uses in our lives as we seek Him and serve Him. But note, as in the life of Moses, and as perfectly displayed in the life of Jesus, it begins with a death to self. It is no wonder that when the Father looked around for someone to encourage His Son on the Mount of Transfiguration that one of those that He turned to was Moses – the selfless servant who served Him in the wilderness.

As Moses here transfers that appointment to Joshua, it is appropriate that we, who are journeying through the wilderness today, ask ourselves if we are prepared and willing to receive just such an appointment. It will only begin with, continue with and end with that same kind of selflessness. That type that Moses evidenced and Jesus spoke of when He said, *"If any of you wants to be My follower, you must put aside your selfish ambition..."* (Luke 9:23).

* * *

46

LIGHT AND TRUTH

"When direction from the LORD is needed, Joshua will stand before Eleazar the priest, who will determine the LORD's will by means of sacred lots. This is how Joshua and the rest of the community of Israel will discover what they should do."
Numbers 27:21

* * *

Joshua was uniquely prepared and divinely appointed to govern a nation and conquer an enemy. Joshua had received great training under Moses and had successfully completed forty years of experience in leading God's people in a subordinate position to Moses. Joshua had been selected by God and was filled with His Spirit; and yet God made it clear that he was to do nothing without first asking for and receiving the counsel of God. God knew that it could be a great temptation, either in his haste or in his own self-confidence, for Joshua to make decisions without first seeking God. In fact, the only times that Joshua failed as a leader during his fifteen year term as their leader were when he failed to seek God's direction (Josh 9:14). God's instruction to Joshua was in essence the same that He has given to you and me: *"trust in the Lord with all your heart; do not depend on your own understanding. Seek His will in ALL you do, and He WILL direct your paths"* (Prov 3:5-6, emphasis added).

Joshua was assured that in every case God would **decide** the course of action to be taken. He would show him the beginning point, the stepping off point and the direction he should go. And God would **direct** the execution of His plan. Nothing would be left to chance or natural order; all would transpire according to God's supernatural order. No detail was too small or too large. As a result, God would **determine** the outcome; and it would be according to His plan, fulfilling His purpose, bringing glory to His Person.

But though Moses had stood face to face before the Lord (Num 12:7-8), Joshua was to stand before the high priest. Though God would not hide His will from Joshua, He would reveal it through the high priest. God would reveal His will through the means of sacred lots. We see these lots described elsewhere in Scripture as "Urim" and Thummim". In Exodus 28:30 we read that the high priest was to insert the Urim and Thummim into the pocket of the chestpiece that he wore, and thus they would be carried over his heart as he went before the Lord in the Holy Place. Thus the high priest *"will always carry the objects used to determine the LORD's will for His people whenever he goes in before the LORD."* The Urim and Thummim were then to be used to determine the will of God when His direction was not clearly understood. Probably they were each marked in some way to indicate "yes" and "no". Then, when thrown, if they both came up "yes" or both came up "no", that was an indication of God's will for that situation. It is this very practice that the writer of Proverbs speaks of: *"We may throw the dice, but the LORD determines how they fall"* (Prov 16:33).

Now before you scurry off to search the internet to see where you can obtain those "dice" to know God's will for all of your decisions in the future, i have good news for you - you already have them in your possession. The word "Urim" means "light"; the word "Thummim" means "truth". The psalmist wrote, *"Your word is a lamp for my feet and a light for my path"* (Psa 119:105). Jesus said, *"If you abide in My word… you shall know the truth"* (John 8:31-32). God's Word is your Urim (light) and Thummim (truth). He has given us His Word that we might know Him, and in knowing Him, know His will. Like Joshua, we are to seek the LORD through His high priest; but our high priest is the High Priest – Jesus (Heb 4:14-16). And though our High Priest, as the Son of Man, knows our weaknesses; as the Son of God, He is blameless (Heb 7:26) and is able to direct us perfectly. We can be assured with even greater confidence than Joshua had, that if we approach God the Father through our High Priest (God the Son), He will clearly and definitively reveal His will. We will confidently know His decision, His direction and His determination for our lives.

. . .

And like Joshua, God has placed us on this journey through the wilderness so that through us He might lead others to experience the victory that He has already accomplished over the enemy. Do i hear you saying, "But I could never be a Joshua"? Joshua was not chosen for his abilities; Joshua was chosen for his availability. He did not accomplish anything because of his greatness; all that was accomplished was through the greatness and the goodness of God. If you protest your ability to be used by God out of some sense of false humility or inadequacy, you are in fact protesting God's ability, which is faithlessness and blasphemy. If God has chosen you, who are you to question Him?

The time has come on your journey. You have been uniquely prepared and divinely appointed. Do nothing without first seeking and then receiving the counsel of God. And then go forth boldly and confidently, walking in His Light and His Truth. There are people to lead, enemies to be conquered and lands to be possessed!

* * *

47

VENGEANCE OR VICTORY?

Then the LORD said to Moses, "Take vengeance on the Midianites for leading the Israelites into idolatry. After that, you will die and join your ancestors." So Moses said to the people, "Choose some men to fight the LORD's war of vengeance against Midian. From each tribe of Israel, send one thousand men into battle." So they chose one thousand men from each tribe of Israel, a total of twelve thousand men armed for battle. Then Moses sent them out, a thousand men from each tribe, and Phinehas son of Eleazar the priest led them into battle. They carried along the holy objects of the sanctuary and the trumpets for sounding the charge. They attacked Midian just as the LORD had commanded Moses, and they killed all the men. All five of the Midianite kings -- Evi, Rekem, Zur, Hur, and Reba -- died in the battle. They also killed Balaam son of Beor with the sword.
Numbers 31:1-8

* * *

This is one of God's last commissions to Moses. He is about to transfer his role of leadership to Joshua, but God directs Moses to send out the people to carry out His judgment. Matthew Henry wrote, *"God sometimes removes useful men when we think they can be ill spared; but this ought to satisfy us, that they are never removed till they have done the work which was appointed them."*

You will recall that God had not promised the land of the Midianites to the Israelites. The Midianites were "worry-free" until they decided to conspire with the Moabites against the Israelites through Balaam. And when the first plan to curse the Israelites failed, they initiated "plan B" – the plan of temptation. God had punished His people for yielding to the temptation of the Midianites; now He would punish the Midianites for tempting His people. God's first response will always be to His people; but He will never let His enemies go unpunished. That is why He would remind us through Paul, *"Dear friends, never avenge yourselves. Leave that to God. For it is written, 'I will take vengeance; I will repay those who deserve it,' says the Lord"* (Rom 12:19).

God did not intend to send out an overwhelming force. The temptation of the Midianites though directed towards God's people was in fact an affront to the Lord God Jehovah. He would punish them for their sin. The size of the force that God chose to use – only one thousand men from each tribe – underlined the fact that this was His battle. Though He would send out a small army, it would be He who defeated the enemy. It is worthy to note that just as God raised His hand of punishment upon the Midianites, at the same time He kept His hand of protection upon the Israelites. Though every Midianite man was killed, not one of the Israelites perished in the battle (Num 32:49).

Look at who God chose to lead the Israelites into battle. He did not choose Joshua, their new leader who had previously led the people to victory on the battlefield; He chose Phinehas, the man He had chosen to be the next high priest. This would not be a military battle; this would be a spiritual battle. They carried the holy objects of the sanctuary. Attention is not given to weapons of military warfare, rather weapons of spiritual warfare. They carried the ark, representing God's presence, and its contents representing His promise of protection, provision and power on behalf of His people. And they carried the trumpets for sounding the charge – the trumpets that would announce the presence of God and assured the protection of God (Num 10:9).

For us today, Midian is a picture of the world. God had placed His people in the land of Midian for a season until He was ready to lead them into the Promised Land. They were to temporarily dwell in the land; they were only passing through. Midian was not their possession. The Israelite's mistake was not that they dwelt in that world, but as we have already seen that they allowed their hearts to be inhabited by the things of that world. You and i are dwelling in a land right now that is not our home. It is not the Promised Land that God has given us to possess. The choice we must make is, will we allow the darkness of the world to creep into our lives, or will we allow the light of Christ to shine out of our lives? While we dwell in Midian, we will be tempted. Paul confirmed that reality when he wrote, *"But remember that the temptations that come into your life are no different from what others experience. And God is faithful. He will keep the temptation from becoming so strong that you can't stand up against it. When you are tempted, he will show you a way out so that you will not give in to it"* (1 Cor 10:13).

God defeated Midian; He destroyed its kings, including Zur, the father of Cozbi, the Midianite princess who had entered the Israelite camp with Zimri in Numbers 25. God even destroyed its backslidden prophet, Balaam, who had authored the plan of deception to begin with.

So as you journey through the Midian of your wilderness, are you an Israelite that God is leading through the land or are you a Midianite who dwells there? Are you like Zimri who succumbed to the temptation of Cozbi, or are you like Phinehas walking in obedience before God? Are you walking in the darkness of the temptation of Midian, or are you walking in the light and the truth of God's Word? Ultimately the people of Midian will experience the vengeance of God and be destroyed, and the people of Israel will experience the victory of God and cross into the Promised Land. Which one will you be?

* * *

48

WE WOULD RATHER LIVE HERE

Now the tribes of Reuben and Gad owned vast numbers of livestock. So when they saw that the lands of Jazer and Gilead were ideally suited for their flocks and herds, they came to Moses, Eleazar the priest, and the other leaders of the people. They said, "...The LORD has conquered this whole area for the people of Israel. It is ideally suited for all our flocks and herds. If we have found favor with you, please let us have this land as our property instead of giving us land across the Jordan River." ...But we do not want any of the land on the other side of the Jordan. We would rather live here on the east side where we have received our inheritance."

Numbers 32:1-2, 4-5, 19

* * *

Here they were at the penultimate moment before entering the land of God's promise. The tribes of Reuben and Gad, as well as the clans of the tribe of Manasseh, had traveled in the middle of the pack during their forty-year journey through the wilderness. But now they wanted to stop short of the Promised Land and settle here on the east bank. The Promised Land was just ahead and yet they looked around themselves at the wilderness and it was pleasing to them. Over five hundred years earlier Abraham's nephew, Lot, had done the same thing. *"Lot took a long look at the fertile plains of the Jordan Valley in the direction of Zoar. ...Lot chose that land for himself--the Jordan Valley to the east of them"* (Gen 13:10-11). Lot chose the land of Sodom and Gomorrah, and God gave Abraham Canaan.

. . .

These tribes now desired the land that they knew versus the land that they knew not. They desired the land that they could see versus the land that they could not see. They desired the land that had already been conquered versus the land that was yet to be conquered. They desired the land that they could have today versus the land that was their promise of tomorrow. They opted for that "bird in the hand" that conventional wisdom says "is worth two in the bush."

Now let us be quick to acknowledge that the Reubenites, the Gadites and the clans of Manasseh were committed to crossing the Jordan River with their brothers and fighting at their side against the Canaanites. Once they had built fortifications for the safety and safekeeping of their wives, children and possessions, they would lead their fellow Israelites into battle. They would not abandon their brothers, only God's promised inheritance.

How do we know that this wasn't God's plan for them? How do we know that He didn't intend these three tribes to inhabit the land on the east side of the Jordan? First, we know it because of what God said. Just as we saw a moment ago, Lot chose the land east of the Jordan, God gave Abraham Canaan; and the land of Canaan was a part of God's covenant with Abraham. At the burning bush, God again clearly defined the land when He listed the tribes that currently occupied it. In Numbers 34 we see God clearly defining the boundaries of the land that He says, *"I am giving you as a special possession"* (Num 34:2). None of these descriptions included the land on the east side of the Jordan. The second reason we know that this wasn't God's plan is not only what God said, but also what the people said. "We do not want any of the land…. We would rather live here…." At best, that declaration was a rejection of God's promise. In essence they were saying, "God, we know You have promised us a land to possess, but we know better what we need; so thanks, but no thanks, God."

At that moment they placed themselves in a posture similar to the serpent's temptation of Adam and Eve: *"You won't die!" the serpent hissed. "God knows that your eyes will be opened when you eat it. You will become just like God, knowing everything, both good and evil"* (Gen 2:4-5). They placed themselves in a posture of believing that they knew better than God what was best for them. Have you ever thought about how disheartening our wrong choices must be to God? He has given us a promise – a promise of His best – a promise that we clearly know; and yet we choose to disregard Him and His promise and go our own way.

• • •

i said earlier that at best it was a rejection of God's promise, because it also could have been a distrust of God's power. Yes, these tribes were willing to advance across Jordan but they were going to leave their families and possessions on the east side, out of harm's way. God's promise may have been well-intentioned in their eyes, but like their fathers before them they questioned God's ability to defeat the giants and subdue the land. They didn't trust God enough to go the distance.

Again i wonder, why did God go along with their plan? Why did He allow them to reject His promise and go their own way? Because God gave them the choice, just like He gives us a choice. We too can choose to follow Him, to trust Him and to stand on His promises; or we can choose to go our own way. And when we choose to go our own way, the seeds of destruction are sown in our choice. In this case, God had chosen and called unto Himself a people. And now a portion of that people was separating unto themselves, and sowing seeds of separation and disunity among the tribe.

God has given you a promise. He has led you on this journey in the fulfillment of His promise. Do not settle for less than He intends. Do not stop on the east side of Jordan. Go all the way, and experience all that He has for you.

* * *

49

TAKE NO PRISONERS

While they were camped near the Jordan River on the plains of Moab opposite Jericho, the LORD said to Moses, "Speak to the Israelites and tell them: 'When you cross the Jordan River into the land of Canaan, you must drive out all the people living there. You must destroy all their carved and molten images and demolish all their pagan shrines. Take possession of the land and settle in it, because I have given it to you to occupy. You must distribute the land among the clans by sacred lot and in proportion to their size. A larger inheritance of land will be allotted to each of the larger clans, and a smaller inheritance will be allotted to each of the smaller clans. The decision of the sacred lot is final. In this way, the land will be divided among your ancestral tribes. But if you fail to drive out the people who live in the land, those who remain will be like splinters in your eyes and thorns in your sides. They will harass you in the land where you live. And I will do to you what I had planned to do to them.' "

Numbers 33:50-56

* * *

J. Vernon McGee said *"God took the Israelites out of Egypt in one night but it took God forty years to get Egypt out of them."* And God's "washing machine" was the wilderness. In the wilderness, the Israelites were separated from the rest of the world. They were isolated from those things that would otherwise distract them or tempt them. While God was using time and experience to purify them from the inside out; He was using the separation in the wilderness to create the time and space in which this transformation could take place. Just like the Israelites, there are things we will not learn in Egypt. Too often, we are at a place in our spiritual walk that the temptations of Egypt are too great and God must take us into the wilderness to remove us from those temptations and remove their hold on us; all the while He is transforming us from the inside out.

But now, that work having been accomplished, it was time for the Israelites to leave the wilderness and enter the Promised Land. Remember, the wilderness was God's preparation; it was not the end of the journey. God didn't say, "IF you cross the Jordan"; He said, "WHEN you cross the Jordan." We would benefit to remember that – the days of the wilderness will come to an end; the land He has promised is ahead and this time of separation will be over. And like the Israelites, God is giving us instruction on the adjustments we must make as we enter into the land – adjustments that will insure our health and life – spiritually, physically and abundantly.

First, they were not only to drive out all the people living there, they were also to destroy and demolish their objects of idol worship and temptation. Every remnant and every object must be obliterated; nothing was to remain, no matter how minor, that could be a reminder of their idolatry. Though those objects were totally acceptable to the Canaanites, they were not acceptable to God for His people. As you enter your promised land it will mean tearing down those high places and destroying the objects of worship of the gods of this world – the god of lust, the god of addiction, the god of materialism, et al. Didn't God allow them to keep just a little bit – because "surely a little bit won't hurt anything"? No! He said destroy it all!

Second, God would give them possession of the land by degree. As they defeated and destroyed the inhabitants and their idolatry, they would gain possession of that portion of the land. God did not intend for them to conquer all of the land at once; it would be a process. So is it true of us. But neither was there anything that the Israelites needed to learn from the current inhabitants about how to possess the land; defeat and destruction must be immediate without any hesitation. There is nothing to be gained from hesitation. The Israelite's obedience was to be swift and deliberate. This may mean for you as you enter your land of promise that you can no longer be around your former "Canaanite friends." God did not tell the Israelites to try to convert them or reform them; He told them to destroy them. You will need to amputatively separate yourself from the Canaanites of your past – IMMEDIATELY, with no hesitation and no exceptions.

. . .

Third, God told them that if they spared the idolater or the idol, their punishment would equal their sin. Anything that they allowed to remain would at some point cause them to be tempted, and that temptation would ultimately lead to death. He made it very clear that any sin that they did not drive out of the land would ultimately turn right around and drive the Israelites out. The reality in their lives, as well as ours, is as Matthew Henry said, *"If we do not put to death our lusts, our lusts will put to death our souls."* The history of the Israelites is replete with examples of idolaters and idols that were not destroyed and the death and destruction that Israel suffered as a result. But that same truth is frequently evident in our own lives. Instances where we have stopped just short of destroying all of the idols or failed to separate ourselves from all of the objects of temptation, and have found ourselves ensnared in sin and death.

As God prepares to lead you into the promised land, heed this lesson. You have not become some kind of "spiritual superman" as a result of your time in the wilderness. Defeat and destroy every remnant of the idolater or its idols. Take no prisoners! And excuse nothing with the thought, "I have never been tempted by that idol before." Remember it's only one step to stupid for every one of us; destroy every remnant and possess the land.

* * *

50

UNCOMMONLY CHOSEN

And the LORD said to Moses, "These are the men who are to divide the land among the people: Eleazar the priest and Joshua son of Nun. Also enlist one leader from each tribe to help them with the task. These are the tribes and the names of the leaders:

Tribe: Leader
Judah: Caleb, son of Jephunneh
Simeon: Shemuel, son of Ammihud
Benjamin: Elidad, son of Kislon
Dan: Bukki, son of Jogli
Manasseh: Hanniel, son of Ephod
Ephraim: Kemuel, son of Shiphtan
Zebulun: Elizaphan, son of Parnach
Issachar: Paltiel, son of Azzan
Asher : Ahihud, son of Shelomi
Naphtali: Pedahel, son of Ammihud

These are the men the LORD has appointed to oversee the dividing of the land of Canaan among the Israelites."
Numbers 34:16-29

* * *

It is easy to skip over this list of names. For one thing, they're hard to pronounce; and for another, we want to get to the "good stuff". But let's stop and look at the "good stuff" right here.

. . .

This "committee" replaces the committee of twelve chosen thirty-eight years before; the committee that foolishly voted ten to two against God's plan and destined the people to wander and die in the wilderness. Caleb, the only incumbent member of the first committee who is still alive is listed first, as its chairman. Joshua has been promoted to be the new leader of the nation, so his seat representing the tribe of Ephraim has been reassigned to Kemuel. And the purview of this committee has now been significantly narrowed. They are not responsible for any feasibility studies or land exploration. They collectively have become the "land apportionment committee". Their job, under the leadership of Eleazar and Joshua, is to insure that the land is divided among the people fairly in accordance with the Lord's instructions.

There are now ten seats on the committee. Since the tribes of Reuben and Gad have chosen to inhabit the land on the east side of the Jordan, they have no say in the apportionment of the Promised Land and therefore are not represented. And though some of the clans of the tribe of Manasseh have chosen to do the same, the remainder will inhabit God's promised land, and therefore those will be represented by Hanniel. You will notice that other than Caleb, none of the leaders that have been chosen are immediate family members of their predecessors on the committee. Remember that they had been men of prestige and position, and so would their families have been. But not only did those men die in the wilderness due to their faithlessness, but also their immediate descendants were divested of their right to serve.

This was a committee that had been groomed in the wilderness for this place of service. It is interesting to note the meaning of their names. Beginning with Shemuel and following the order that their names are recorded in the passage through Pedahel, their names meant: heard by God, loved by God, proven by God, graced by God, assembled by God, concealed by God, delivered by God, honored by God and redeemed by God. What a pedigree for a committee! (One quick side road while we are looking at names: Ammihud, the father of Shemuel of the tribe of Simeon, and Ammihud, the father of Pedahel of the tribe of Naphtali, are not the same person. Apparently it was a common name in that day, but it had an uncommon meaning – "people of glory". Oh, that we might be a "people of glory" through which our Lord's glory is conspicuously reflected as we journey through our wilderness!)

. . .

So what is the application for us today? The application comes in the contrast of the two committees. Both groups were called by God and chosen for a specific task in accordance with His purpose. Both groups were uniquely equipped and uniquely gifted. But the first group was known for their personal and individual achievements – their strengths and successes. The second group was known for who they were in God. The first group became disoriented by their own wisdom and understanding. The second group was prepared to seek and to follow God's wisdom and His direction. The greatest weakness of the first group was their personal identities and the greatest strength of the second group was their identity in the Lord.

God has allowed you to journey through the crucible of the wilderness. During that time He has heard you, He has loved you, He has tested and proven you, He has bestowed His grace upon you, He has assembled you, He has concealed and protected you, He has delivered you, He has honored you as His child, and He has redeemed you. You are now uniquely prepared to follow Him and to be used by Him. Very soon, you will enter His land of promise. Go forth in His wisdom, His strength and His direction. You are His child, and you have been uncommonly chosen.

* * *

51

A PLACE OF REFUGE

"You must give the Levites six cities of refuge, where a person who has accidentally killed someone can flee for safety. In addition, give them forty-two other towns."...And the LORD said to Moses, "...Designate six cities of refuge for yourselves, three on the east side of the Jordan River and three on the west in the land of Canaan. These cities are for the protection of Israelites, resident foreigners, and traveling merchants. Anyone who accidentally kills someone may flee there for safety. ...But if the slayer leaves the city of refuge, and the victim's nearest relative finds him outside the city limits and kills him, it will not be considered murder. The slayer should have stayed inside the city of refuge until the death of the high priest. But after the death of the high priest, the slayer may return to his own property. ...You must not defile the land where you are going to live, for I live there myself. I am the LORD, who lives among the people of Israel."
Numbers 35:6, 9, 13-15, 26-28, 34

* * *

The Lord gave forty-eight cities to the tribe of Levi throughout all of the land, including the land on the east side of the Jordan. Among those were six cities that would be designated as "cities of refuge". Webster's Dictionary describes a refuge as "a stronghold which protects by its strength, or a sanctuary which secures safety by its sacredness." God established the cities of refuge to specifically deal with the act of murder. In doing so, He established two foundational truths about the sin of murder. First, the sin of murder not only defiles the murderer, but also the land. If God was going to dwell among His people, He could not dwell among a defiled people in a defiled land. Therefore the sin of murder, just as the sin of any kind, could not go unpunished or unredeemed. And He established that redemption could only come through the shedding of blood; it could not be bought with wealth or works. Therefore He established that intentional murder must be punished through the execution of the murderer by the nearest relative of the victim. Punishment and redemption were not optional; there was no protection from willful murder.

God established the cities of refuge to protect those who had accidentally killed someone else. Pending trial a murderer could surrender to a city of refuge, where he would be judged. If the slaying was determined not to be willful, the slayer could live in the city of refuge without fear of retribution. The slayer would live out his life there until death or until the death of the currently serving high priest, at which time the slayer would be free to leave the city of refuge as an innocent man.

These cities of refuge are a picture for us of our Lord Jesus Christ. He is our Refuge. He is our Stronghold who protects by His strength, and our Sanctuary who secures by His sacredness. The cities were situated throughout the land in such a way that no matter where you were situated, you were within a half-day's journey of a city of refuge. Refuge was within the immediate access of everyone. The psalmist wrote, "*God is our refuge and strength, a very present help in trouble*" (Psa 46:1 NKJ). The proximity of the cities is a picture that refuge is within everyone's grasp.

Second, as long as a slayer stayed within the boundaries of a city of refuge, he was safe from condemnation or retribution. As such, this is the picture that the apostle Paul had in mind when he wrote, "*There is therefore now no condemnation to those who are in Christ Jesus*" (Rom 8:1 NKJ). Within the safety and sanctuary of Christ there is no condemnation.

The third picture is that sinners are welcome. The cities of refuge were not established for righteous men, but for sinners. There they would receive counsel and ministry extended by grace. Jesus Himself said, "*For the Son of Man has come to seek and to save that which was lost*" (Luke 19:10 NKJ). Jesus came to be a refuge for sinners.

The fourth picture is that all were welcome. The cities of refuge were not only for the people of Israel, but also for foreigners and travelers. All that entered into its gates by faith would find refuge. Our Lord came to bring redemption and refuge to every tongue, every tribe and every people.

The fifth picture is that the cities of refuge provided refuge not due to the physical strength of their walls, but by the appointment of God, and refuge could only come through His means. Refuge did not exist outside of those boundaries, only within. Just as we will find refuge in Christ as we abide in Him.

The last parallel we need to see is the governance of the cities of refuge. These were cities under the control of the tribe of Levi. The Levites served God and the people under the authority of the High Priest. The High Priest, as he lived made atonement for the sins of the people, including those seeking refuge within those cities; and upon his death atonement and redemption were considered to be paid in full; the slayers were free to go. Through the death of our High Priest, Jesus, our redemption was made complete and through His resurrection we have been granted eternal and abundant life – our debt has been paid in full, we are free to walk in everlasting life with Him.

As we journey through the wilderness with Christ, we journey as those who have found refuge – our strength and security. We need not flee to a city; we need but to abide in Him. Walk today in that confidence, that assurance, and that hope – that only comes through our Place of Refuge, our Lord and Savior, Jesus Christ.

* * *

52

REMEMBER YOUR HISTORY, DON'T REPEAT IT

This book records the words that Moses spoke to all the people of Israel while they were in the wilderness east of the Jordan River. They were camped in the Jordan Valley near Suph, between Paran on one side and Tophel, Laban, Hazeroth, and Di-zahab on the other. Normally it takes only eleven days to travel from Mount Sinai to Kadesh-barnea, going by way of Mount Seir. But forty years after the Israelites left Mount Sinai, on a day in midwinter, Moses gave these speeches to the Israelites, telling them everything the LORD had commanded him to say.
Deuteronomy 1:1-3

* * *

A journey that should have taken eleven days took forty years. Talk about a detour! And as the people at long last stood with anticipation at the point of entering God's Promised Land, Moses addressed the people. After forty years in the wilderness, what would Moses say? Knowing that he would be leaving this people to cross into the land without him, what words of challenge would he give them that would carry them into the land?

Some of us might have been tempted to affirm the people for their perseverance. They had endured forty years in the wilderness with all of its hardships and challenges. They had experienced the grief of seeing an entire generation die in the wilderness. They had traveled for extended periods without the availability of fresh water. Many of them had grown up in the wilderness with no place to call home. And through it all they had persevered; surely Moses would speak words of affirmation to them.

Others of us may have chosen to rally the people to courageously advance to create and build a nation for their children and their children's children; a place they could call home, a place where they would be master and not slave, and a place that would be safe and secure for their future generations. Perhaps Moses would outline the military strategy that they would follow to insure victory over the inhabitants of the land. Surely these would be words that would rival any ever spoken by a commander as he led his troops into battle; Moses would speak words of honor and of courage to them.

Perhaps Moses would celebrate the military victories of days gone by. He would recall their recent defeat of the Midianites without the loss of a single Israelite life. He would recall the rout of the giants of Bashan, and the victory over Sihon, king of Heshbon. Surely Moses would boast of their military might.

But alas no, rather Moses reminded them of the faithlessness of their fathers. He reminded them of the faithless report of the ten spies and the murmuring and complaining of the people. He reminded them of their feeble attempt to disobey God and enter the land after God had commanded them to turn back to the wilderness. He reminded them of the thirty-eight years of wandering that had resulted from their faithless disobedience.

And he reminded them, that despite that faithlessness, God had been faithful through it all. He recounted God's provision, His protection and His proficiency. He rehearsed His favor, His grace and His mercy.

He then challenged them to walk in the fear of the Lord, confident in the favor of the Lord. It was a moment of history remembered so that it would not be an era of history to be repeated. The Lord had again set the land before them. Moses was admonishing them not to repeat the sins of their fathers and once more be turned away.

Approximately fourteen hundred years later Jesus told the crowd that followed Him, "*If any of you wants to be My follower, you must put aside your selfish ambition, shoulder your cross daily, and follow Me.*" "*But don't begin until you count the cost. For who would begin construction of a building without first getting estimates and then checking to see if there is enough money to pay the bills?*" (Luke 9:23; 14:28) Oswald Chambers wrote, "*Our Lord was not referring here to a cost which we have to count, but to a cost which He has already counted*" – a cost that He has paid. As the Israelites stood at the boundary of the Promised Land, Moses was reminding them that the land would come at a cost – battles against giants and fortified cities; but that the Lord God Jehovah would enable them to pay the cost. He would go with them to fight for them. He would tear down the walls. He would give them the strategy. He would enable them to fight victoriously. Yes, He would give them favor.

As you draw closer to the land of God's promise for you, you too can be confident of the favor of your Lord. Recite His promise. Do not add to what the Lord has said, and do not subtract from it. Recall His faithfulness, even in your times of faithlessness. Recount His provision and protection throughout the journey. He has counted the cost. Don't allow yourself to be an obstacle in His way. Get out of the way. Then hold on tight and walk with Him His way! Rehearse the lessons He has taught you in the wilderness. As you enter into the land, do not forget them. Allow this moment of history remembered to be a reminder in the days to come, so that they not be the days of history repeated.

* * *

53

TEACH YOUR CHILDREN WELL

"These are all the commands, laws, and regulations that the LORD your God told me to teach you so you may obey them in the land you are about to enter and occupy.... Hear, O Israel! The LORD is our God, the LORD alone. And you must love the LORD your God with all your heart, all your soul, and all your strength. And you must commit yourselves wholeheartedly to these commands I am giving you today. Repeat them again and again to your children. Talk about them when you are at home and when you are away on a journey, when you are lying down and when you are getting up again. Tie them to your hands as a reminder, and wear them on your forehead. Write them on the doorposts of your house and on your gates."

Deuteronomy 6:1, 4-9

* * *

"Hear, O Israel, YAHWEH is Elohim, He is One." In that brief statement, God gave revelation of Himself and confirmed His triune nature. As YAHWEH, He revealed His eternality, without beginning and without end. As Elohim, He revealed His plurality as Father, Son and Spirit. And in His statement that the LORD is one alone, He revealed His unity as the Sovereign Almighty All-sufficient God. He commanded that we as His children are in turn to love Him with a sincere love (a love of the heart), a superlative love (an unequaled love of the soul) and a strong love (a love that is unconditional and unending). As their (and our) Heavenly Father He had repeatedly demonstrated His wholehearted love for His children and now He commanded that they commit themselves to Him wholeheartedly – not only in their own practice, but also in training the generations to come. God has no grandchildren, only children that are wholly-committed to Him. And He charges His children with the responsibility of teaching, training and nurturing His next generation of children. He commanded the children of Israel to teach their children well.

The responsibility for teaching and training their children in the admonition of the Lord could not be abdicated to anyone else. Though professional teachers and priests may have been a part of the process, the responsibility remained with the parents. God commanded them to teach their children through formal instruction, repeating God's words to them. For them to know God's heart and His character, they must know His Word and His commands. They must hear God's Word spoken through the mouths of the parents – not only on special days, but on every day. They must know that God's Word is a lamp to their feet and a light to their path. Is it no wonder that many today walk blindly off the path because they have never or seldom heard the word of light spoken in their home?

But God not only commanded them to formally instruct, He also told them to teach their children through informal instruction, demonstrating God's words through their actions. They were to model God's Word in their homes, as well as when they were away, while they were lying down, as well as when they were getting up. In other words they were to reflect God's Word through their actions and their lifestyles at ALL times. Teaching was not only to come by the spoken word; it must be lived out through action. Truth cannot only be taught by speaking it out loud, it must be taught by living it out loud. The sermon that truly lasts is not the one spoken on Sunday morning; it is the one that is modeled on Monday morning and throughout the week. God was clearly instructing the Israelites that their walk must align with their talk; both are necessary and both must point to Him.

Not only was God's word to direct their steps and their stops, their comings and their goings, it was to be tied to their hands and worn on their foreheads. It was to govern their labor and their thoughts, their activities and their attitudes, and their worship – in deed and in word. This command subsequently led the children of Israel to implement the practice of wearing a phylactery – a small square box worn on the head and left arm which contained slips of parchment on which were written the commands of God. This was to signify obedience to this command.

• • •

Lastly, God's word was to be conspicuous in their lives and their homes. He told them to display His word on the doorposts and gateposts of their homes. Every person entering their home and their gates was to know that they were children of the Living God, set apart for His purpose. A second religious practice which was implanted by the Jews as a result of this command was the use of the Mezuzah – a scroll of parchment inscribed with this passage (Deut 6:4-9) and the command to love God and serve Him found in Deuteronomy 11:13-21. The Mezuzah is encased in an ornamental covering and affixed to the upper third of the right door post in a slanted position with the top pointed toward the inside of the room, to signify the sanctity and blessing of the Jewish home. Jesus would one day denounce the Pharisees for their legalistic observance of God's commands through outward symbols such as these without any evidence of the truth and spirit of God's commands being reflected through their lives (Matt 23:2-12). God's command was not for outward symbols, it was for their hearts to be set apart and surrendered to Him.

As we journey through our wilderness, our Lord has commanded us to teach our children well – to reflect His Word, His Truth and His character in our every thought, attitude and action. Do not lose sight of this command. God's lessons for you in this wilderness are not only for you, they are for those who come behind you – beginning with your children. Jesus said, *"Go and make disciples… teaching them to obey all the commands I have given you"* (Matt 28:19-20). Teach your children; teach them well.

* * *

54

THE TRIAL OF PROSPERITY

"The LORD your God will soon bring you into the land he swore to give your ancestors Abraham, Isaac, and Jacob. It is a land filled with large, prosperous cities that you did not build. The houses will be richly stocked with goods you did not produce. You will draw water from cisterns you did not dig, and you will eat from vineyards and olive trees you did not plant. When you have eaten your fill in this land, be careful not to forget the LORD, who rescued you from slavery in the land of Egypt."

Deuteronomy 6:10-12

* * *

Throughout your time in the wilderness, you've experienced God's provision and protection through the trials. Yes, God has provided for your needs, and He has provided miraculously, but in many instances He has not provided for your "wants". Perhaps as you have journeyed through this wilderness, you have looked at those around you who are experiencing prosperity and wondered when your opportunity will come. Perhaps as you've slept on the straw mat in your tent, you've longed for the cushiony mattress on the four-poster bed. Perhaps as you've eaten the manna of heaven, you've longed for the fresh grapes from the vineyard. Perhaps as you've experienced thirst on the journey, you've longed for the fresh cool water of your own cistern. Or perhaps you've tried to push those desires out of your mind for fear that you are being shallow or ungrateful to God.

. . .

God had promised the Israelites a land flowing with milk and honey. He had delighted in His servant Abraham when He told him, *"Take a walk in very direction and explore the new possessions I am giving you"* (Gen 13:17). He had promised to lead His children *"into their own good and spacious land"* (Ex 3:8). He didn't promise them mediocrity; He promised them His best. And Jesus reminded them over 1400 years later, *"If you sinful people know how to give good gifts to your children, how much more will your Heavenly Father give good gifts to those who ask Him"* (Matt 7:11) Oh, and incidentally, this "7-Eleven" (Matt 7:11) never closes, is never out of stock and only delivers the Father's best.

And now after forty years in the wilderness, literally a lifetime for some, God was preparing them to receive their inheritance – the fruit of His promise. They were about to receive and experience all the things they had lacked in the wilderness. They were about to inhabit cities and houses they did not build, enjoying goods and furnishings they did not produce, while they satisfied their thirst with water from wells they did not dig and dined on fresh fruits and vegetables from gardens they did not plant. And it was not going to be just enough to get by; God was going to provide for them to their "fill". What they had lacked in the wilderness, they would luxuriate in once they inhabited the Promised Land. But God knew their propensity – just as He knows ours. He knew that their dependence upon Him in the wilderness could well be forgotten in the prosperity of the Promised Land. He knew that the curse of blessings is, that all too often, we forget or neglect the Giver of those blessings. And He admonished them to be careful not to forget. The writer in Proverbs also struggled with the trial of blessings when he wrote, *"Give me neither poverty nor riches! Give me just enough to satisfy my needs. For if I grow rich, I may deny you and say, 'Who is the LORD?' And if I am too poor, I may steal and thus insult God's holy name"* (Prov 30:8-9).

Now lest i leave you with the impression that God promises that every wilderness journey will conclude with the realization of this world's material wealth – that is not the case! But if we are faithful in our pursuit of Him, each journey will conclude with the realization of God's promised blessings. The truth to grasp and hold onto is that what God has promised He will provide; what He has revealed we will realize. But during this time in the wilderness He has allowed you to journey in a state of desperate dependence on Him – your circumstances and surroundings in the midst of the journey have necessitated it. He has allowed it in order to bring you to a greater understanding of Who He is and a greater realization of your dependence on Him. Now comes the really hard part – maintaining that level of desperate dependence when the circumstances that caused it have been removed – and even more, been replaced by times of prosperity that lull us into a false sense of security in ourselves and our surroundings, and blind us to our dependence on the One Who led us through the wilderness.

While we are still in that state of desperate dependence in the wilderness, it is easy to say, "Lord, I won't forget." It's not unlike Peter, when He said to Jesus, *"Not even if I have to die with you! I will never deny you!"* (Mark 14:31) Now before you resign yourself by thinking, "If Peter could blow it that bad what chance do I have?" – let us look at what Jesus said to him just before that. *"Satan has asked to sift you like wheat. But I have pleaded in prayer for you that your faith should not fail"* (Luke 22:31-32).

You, like the Israelites, are about to face the trial of prosperity, and Jesus is interceding on your behalf that your faith should not fail. Do not forget what He has done. Do not forget the slavery from which He has rescued you. As you inhabit the city, or live in the house, or drink from the well, or eat from the garden *"look to the rock from which you were hewn, and to the hole of the pit from which you were dug"* (Isa 51:1 NKJ). And look to the One Who has been faithful through it all.

* * *

55

A LITTLE WHILE

"When the LORD your God brings you into the land you are about to enter and occupy, he will clear away many nations ahead of you…."
Deuteronomy 7:1

* * *

As the Israelites make their preparations to enter into the land, i want us to stop and reflect. Perhaps like me you are not yet at the place in your journey that your land of promise is in sight. So let's look at the lesson here.

What do you do in the wilderness for forty years? How do you wander for forty years in a space of land that can be traversed in eleven days? How do you fill your days? How do you maintain your sanity? How do you persevere without abandoning the promises of God? How do you continue on day after day without discouragement taking hold?

As i sit here writing these words, i am mindful that the Lord has slowed down the pace of my journey through this wilderness. Things i was able to write in a single day when i began this journey some months ago, now take an entire week. The thoughts and the words don't come as quickly. There is greater labor to compose a thought. Though i sense His anointing as much as i did then, i can see how He has slowed my pace. The enthusiasm and excitement that i enjoyed in those early days of this journey have ebbed. i sometimes wonder now if i will ever come to the end of this journey. Don't misunderstand me; i know the promises that God has given me. i know that He is faithful. i know that in His time, He will bring it about. Peter's words echo in my mind: *"In His kindness God called you to His eternal glory by means of Jesus Christ. After you have suffered a little while, He will restore, support, and strengthen you, and He will place you on a firm foundation"* (1 Pet 5:10) i know that day will come, but even with that knowledge, i have grown weary in the journey.

i guess my difficulty stems from my definition of "a little while" versus God's definition. And though i know He looks from the framework of eternity, my finite mind is having difficulty looking beyond next week. And from where i am sitting right now, all i can see in every direction is wilderness. i wish i could see the Promised Land ahead. i wish i could see the banks of the Jordan approaching. But all i see is wilderness.

Many well-meaning friends ask, "What's happening?" You can tell from the sound of their voice that they are fully expecting to hear an enthusiastic report of God's parting of the Jordan River and our entry into the Promised Land. But the reality is, the journey this week is the same as it was last week, and it's becoming difficult to tell the weeks apart.

i don't want to sound ungrateful. God is providing for us and protecting as we journey. We clearly see His hand of blessing. We see His presence, His provision, even His Person guiding our way. i echo with David that i have been young and i have been old, *"yet I have never seen the godly forsaken, nor seen their children begging for bread"* (Ps 37:25). And i know that in the midst of this journey, God is fulfilling His purpose even when i can't see what it is. But i long to be out of the wilderness. i long to be in that land of milk and honey. i long to put away the garments of the wilderness and put on the vestments of the Promised Land.

As you stand where you are in your journey through the wilderness, what are you feeling? Has it ceased being a journey <u>through</u> the wilderness, and become a journey <u>in</u> the wilderness? Are you feeling disheartened or disgruntled because of all the time that God has "left you" to wander? Are you feeling misused by God for those "lost" days, months or years? Are you feeling forgotten by God? Are you so busy looking at the journey past that you are having difficulty considering the journey ahead?

• • •

If so, i think you are experiencing a glimpse of how the Israelites felt. i think that we can sometimes be a little harsh on them as we look back at them from our easy chairs. As we look at the mighty works of God on their behalf and yet see them disobey time and again, i think we can miss the effects of walking in their sandals for forty years.

But that is when we must recall that the time in the wilderness *"produces perseverance; and perseverance, character; and character, hope. Now hope does not disappoint…."* (Rom 5:3-5 NKJ). And our Lord will not cause us to endure any longer than is necessary to produce that perseverance. The potter, after he has shaped the clay into a pot, uses time and temperature to harden it and prepare it for use. Our Potter has His hand on the timer and the temperature control. The "heat" of the wilderness will be no greater than what He requires; neither will our time in it.

God had given the Israelites this time that they too might be adequately prepared. He had also allowed this time for the benefit of the nations of Canaan, so that rather than being destroyed they might turn from their sin and turn to Him (Gen 15:16). As the Israelites were wandering, God was patiently waiting. He is patiently waiting for us as well.

You too <u>will</u> enter and occupy the land. You are one day closer than you were yesterday. The land lies ahead. Persevere "a little while" longer. The Promised Land lies just on the other side of this wilderness. It's not the distance; it's the timing. And only the Potter controls that!

* * *

56

REMEMBER WHY YOU'RE THERE

"When the LORD your God brings you into the land you are about to enter and occupy, he will clear away many nations ahead of you.... These ... nations are all more powerful than you. When the LORD your God hands these nations over to you and you conquer them, you must completely destroy them. Make no treaties with them and show them no mercy. ...For you are a holy people, who belong to the LORD your God. Of all the people on earth, the LORD your God has chosen you to be his own special treasure. The LORD did not choose you and lavish his love on you because you were larger or greater than other nations, for you were the smallest of all nations! It was simply because the LORD loves you, and because he was keeping the oath he had sworn to your ancestors. ...You will be blessed above all the nations of the earth. None of your men or women will be childless, and all your livestock will bear young. And the LORD will protect you from all sickness."

Deuteronomy 7:1-2, 6-8, 14-15

* * *

What did the Israelites do to deserve the Promised Land? Was it their size or their strength? Was it their intelligence or their might? Was it their hard work or their dedication? Was it their goodness or their greatness? Was it their faithfulness or their godliness? No, time and again they had demonstrated that they were a stiff-necked and an ill-natured people. There was nothing to recommend them or entitle them to the blessings of God. It was simply because the Lord loved them and He was keeping His promise.

. . .

Moses called them a holy people. They were holy, not because of their efforts or their attributes, but because God had set them apart unto Himself. They belonged to God; and in His holiness, anything that belongs to Him has become holy. He has not only established the definition of "holy", it is His very nature. And He had chosen this people to be His own special treasure. Moses was now reminding this people – not of who they were – but Whose they were. He was reminding them that He Who had delivered them from the bondage behind them would give them victory over the nations ahead of them. It would not be a function of their goodness; it would be a function of His grace. It would not be a function of their might; it would be a function of His mercy. It would not be a function of their giftedness; it would be a function of His glory.

God had separated this people unto Himself and He was now reminding them to stay separate. The nations that currently occupied the Promised Land had long ago turned from God; they had abandoned His Person and His ways. They were a people that had turned to immoral indulgences and idolatrous worship. God instructed His people to remain separate from these nations, to utterly destroy them and to make no treaty with them. Righteousness can make no treaty with idolatry. And though the Israelites in and of themselves were not righteous, as God's people they were clothed in His righteousness. God assured them that as they walked in obedience to Him they would experience His blessing above all the nations of the earth. He promised that they and their livestock would be fruitful and multiply, and be protected from illness and destruction.

i wonder what the Israelites were thinking as they heard this promise. Do you think they were focused on the land of milk and honey ahead of them or the journey through the wilderness behind them? Do you think their thoughts were absorbed in the promised blessings ahead or the endured hardships behind? Imagine the excitement that they now sensed as they stood at the concluding edge of their wilderness journey.

God has not called us to our respective journeys based upon our merits either. He isn't leading us to the Promised Land because we deserve it. He is leading us there because He loves us, He has chosen us, and He has called us to be a part of His promise to the nations. We have been adopted into His family through the shed blood of Jesus, and set apart to be His holy people.

• • •

As we enter into the land that He has set before us, we too must remain separate from the people of the land. We are to carry the message of His Good News, but we are to make no treaty. There can be no compromise. We cannot become unequally yoked. God has blessed us above the nations in order to be a blessing to the nations, not to be a part of the nations.

Our victory is assured. God's purpose will be fulfilled; His name will be proclaimed and His Person will be worshipped – not because of who we are, but because of Who He is. When He brings you into the land you are about to enter, remember why He brought you, remember why you're there.

* * *

57

THE PLACE HE CHOOSES

"You must seek the LORD your God at the place he himself will choose from among all the tribes for his name to be honored. Today you are doing whatever you please, but that is not how it will be when you arrive in the place of rest the LORD your God is giving you. You will soon cross the Jordan River and live in the land the LORD your God is giving you as a special possession. When he gives you rest and security from all your enemies, you must bring everything I command you--your burnt offerings, your sacrifices, your tithes, your special gifts, and your offerings to fulfill a vow--to the place the LORD your God will choose for his name to be honored. You must celebrate there with your sons and daughters and all your servants in the presence of the LORD your God. It might happen that the place the LORD your God chooses for his name to be honored is a long way from your home."

Deuteronomy 12:5, 8-12, 21

* * *

Worship is our expression of our love for God, expressed to Him in every way possible through every facet of our lives throughout every moment of our lives. Obedience to Him is an expression of worship. Lifting our voices in praise to Him is an expression of worship. Offering our heartfelt prayers silently to Him is an expression of worship. An act of love extended to another with nothing expected in return is an expression of worship. Worship is the Father's love expressed back to Him. Never get confused that worship is limited to a time and a place on a Saturday night or a Sunday morning. Worship is 24/7. It is not so much an activity as it is an attitude; but worship activity will flow out of an attitude of worship.

Now having said that, don't miss God's command to the Israelites to gather together to worship Him corporately. And as they prepared to enter the Land, God gave them some very clear instruction on how and where.

The writer of the book of Hebrews writes, *"Think of ways to encourage one another to outbursts of love and good deeds. And let us not neglect our meeting together, as some people do, but encourage and warn each other, especially now that the day of his coming back again is drawing near"* (Heb 10:24-25). Our Lord has placed within us that need to gather together with fellow believers to encourage and edify one another. We are His body through which He ministers to a lost and dying world. We are not to be isolated from one another; He has made us to be interdependent with one another. And here the Lord was instructing the people through Moses to gather together to worship Him at a specific place – a place at which they were to present to Him their tithes, their offerings, their gifts and their sacrifices.

First, the Lord made it very clear that it would not be in a place of their choosing; it would be in a place of His choosing. Throughout their time in the wilderness, they had had greater liberty in choosing where they would worship, but once they crossed over the Jordan, He would choose the place. In this day and time, "church-hopping" has become a popular pass time. We tend to leave churches when we feel our "needs" aren't being met, when we don't like the style of music, when we don't like the style of preaching, or when we have been offended in some way or another. Our immediate reaction is to "get out of Dodge" and find another church. And we often look for the church that best meets the "needs" of our family; we look for the church that "feels" right. Now don't misunderstand me, God will use circumstances to confirm His direction in our lives, but too often we allow circumstances to drive our direction for our lives. We discern God's will based upon what seems best to us. And that is what God was instructing His people not to do.

The Lord told them that His place of worship for them might not be the most convenient place. It very well may be "a long way from your home." Distance cannot be the measurement by which we determine the place of worship of which God is directing us to be a part. God never promised that worship should be convenient.

He told them that His place of worship for them might not be the most popular place. Too often we can be distracted by what is new and exciting. We all have a desire to be a part of something that is successful – something that is growing and going. But if we make popularity our criteria for joining a church we will constantly be moving from one place to the next following whatever is the newest or the most exciting. Allow me to hurriedly point out that if we are worshipping God, wherever He has placed us, it will be fresh and new and exciting, because as the prophet Jeremiah wrote, *"Great is His faithfulness; His mercies begin afresh each day"* (Lam 3:23). Popularity cannot be the measurement by which we determine the place of worship to which God is directing us.

Also, it will be the place He chooses – for you – and your entire family. Earlier we saw the Lord's admonition to the parents to train up their children in the Lord's commands. He commands them here to celebrate "with your sons and your daughters". Corporate worship is a family activity. Guard and protect that time together as a family to worship together in that place that He has chosen.

As the Lord brings you to the end of your journey, it could very well be in a new place. Trust Him to lead you to the place that He would have you worship. Remember He chooses the place – His place – not ours.

* * *

58

THE CHOICE IS OURS

Moses summoned all the Israelites and said to them, "You have seen with your own eyes everything the LORD did in Egypt to Pharaoh and all his servants and his whole country-- all the great tests of strength, the miraculous signs, and the amazing wonders. For forty years I led you through the wilderness, yet your clothes and sandals did not wear out. The LORD your God is making this covenant with you who stand in his presence today and also with all future generations of Israel. ...This command I am giving you today is not too difficult for you to understand or perform. It is not up in heaven.... It is not beyond the sea.... The message is very close at hand; it is on your lips and in your heart so that you can obey it. Now listen! Today I am giving you a choice between prosperity and disaster.... ...Today I have given you the choice between life and death, between blessings and curses. I call on heaven and earth to witness the choice you make. Oh, that you would choose life, that you and your descendants might live! Choose to love the LORD your God and to obey him and commit yourself to him, for he is your life...."

Deuteronomy 29:2-3, 5, 15; 30:11-15, 19-20

* * *

Throughout the journey, God had demonstrated His love for His people through tests of strength, miraculous signs and amazing wonders. Even to the detail of the clothes on their back and the sandals on their feet, God demonstrated His care and concern for His children. And today on the plains of Moab, as the people came to the end of their wanderings through the wilderness God was renewing His covenant and defining their choice.

• • •

God would not require of them what they could not give. He was calling them to love Him, obey Him and commit their lives to Him. He would not require of them what they did not understand. His commands would not be so high that they could not grasp them. His commands would not be so deep that they could not fathom them. He would place His commands before them, placing them on their lips and writing them on their hearts. He would not command them to do what they could not perform. What He called them to, He would equip them for. What He called them to begin, He would enable them to complete. What He called them to obey, He would give them the ability to fulfill.

We have an advantage that the Israelites did not; Jesus has come – He has paid the price for our sins. Will we choose to follow Him? And if we are followers of Jesus, He has given us His Holy Spirit to dwell within us. Not only has God given us His Word that we might know the Truth, and given us His Son that we might walk in the Truth, He has given us His Spirit that we might be empowered to walk according to His Truth. But just like the Israelites, He has given us a choice.

PROSPERITY OR DISASTER? *"Trusting the LORD leads to prosperity"* (Prov 28:25). Webster's defines "prosperity" as the "attainment of the object desired". God is not talking about the attainment of "things"; He's talking about the attainment of Him. Without Him we will never be prosperous, no matter what material possessions we may have. Webster's also defines "disaster" as "extreme, usually irremediable, ruin". If prosperity is the attainment of God, disaster is the "falling short" of God, and the ruin that comes from being separated from Him.

LIFE OR DEATH? Jesus came that we might have life – and have it abundantly (John 10:10). Not merely existence, but life to the max – supercharged, superabundant and supernatural. It is life with a purpose, life with a passion and life everlasting. If life is all of those things, then death is its exact opposite – there is no purpose, no passion, and it will not endure. Don't confuse this life with the physical temporal life that we have here on earth. Unless Jesus returns first, this life as we know it will come to an end, and we will experience physical death. But the life God was talking about will not be stopped by physical death, if anything it will be enhanced as we are loosed from the constraints of this earth. The life

God is speaking of here will continue forever - life with Him, life in His presence, and life centered in His purpose.

BLESSINGS OR CURSES? "Blessing" is experiencing the fullness of what our Heavenly Father has for us. It is walking in His goodness and His love, experiencing His mercy and His grace. Though "curses" may include injury that may come upon us as a result of disobedience, the greater curse is the absence of walking in His goodness and His love. It is the failure to experience His mercy and His grace. i can think of no greater curse, no greater feeling of aloneness, than walking apart from Him.

And God said He was calling on heaven and earth to witness their choice. He surrounded them as He has surrounded us with *"a huge crowd of witnesses to the life of faith"* (Heb 12:1). Imagine yourself standing in the center of a huge coliseum, as in days of old. You are standing with other men and women in the first century, who, like you, are about to be martyred for their faith in Christ. But this stadium is not crowded with maniacal Romans who are cheering for your blood and your death; rather, it is an assemblage of men and women who have gone before us and finished well. As you look up into the gallery, these men and women begin to walk in and take their seats. First come Abraham and Sarah, followed by Isaac and Joseph and Daniel. Somewhere in the crowd are Queen Esther and Ruth and Rahab. Peter and Paul followed by the rest of the apostles soon make their entry. You see people like William Carey, Hudson Taylor, Jonathan Edwards and Corrie Ten Boom. And soon the stadium is full to capacity. Then from their midst steps Jesus. And you are overcome by the love He is expressing toward you through His countenance and His words. And as if in one voice He leads this gathering in a prayer of intercession for you. And as you keep your eyes on Him, He enables you to finish well – He enables you to make the right choice. He enables you to choose life.

The Father has given us His promise, a future and a hope. Here on this plain of Moab of your journey He has renewed His promise to you. He's been faithful throughout the journey past. He will be faithful in the journey ahead, wherever it leads. But the choice is ours. *"Choose to love the LORD your God and to obey Him and commit yourself to Him, for He is your life…."*

* * *

59

BE STRONG AND COURAGEOUS

Then Moses called for Joshua, and as all Israel watched he said to him, "Be strong and courageous! For you will lead these people into the land that the LORD swore to give their ancestors. You are the one who will deliver it to them as their inheritance. Do not be afraid or discouraged, for the LORD is the one who goes before you. He will be with you; he will neither fail you nor forsake you."
Deuteronomy 31:7-8

* * *

Moses had been the undershepherd of this people for forty years. He was the one through whom God had led this people through the wilderness in times of plenty, times of victory and times of faithfulness. But God didn't call him to lead only in the good times; he was the leader even when the people rebelled – even when they were experiencing times of scarcity, times of defeat, and times of faithlessness. He heard their complaints and their murmurings. He was the recipient of frequent criticism. As the need arose he was their advocate, their mediator, their judge, their disciplinarian, their teacher, their pastor, their general, their leader and their friend. No one knew the responsibilities that Joshua was about to assume better than Moses. No other man truly understood the weight of the burden of responsibility that he was about to shoulder.

Now before you correct me – i know that God was the Leader of the people. i know that the responsibility and the burden was God's. And i know that we are called to lay down our burdens upon Him. But Jesus did say, *"Take My yoke upon you.... My yoke fits perfectly, and the burden I give you is light"* (Matt 11:29-30). Our Lord takes the weight of that responsibility, but if we are going to take up His cross and follow Him, there is a burden. And He has promised that He will enable us to bear that burden. And He will never give us a burden that He will not enable us to bear.

With that understanding, Moses called for Joshua to give him his final words of instruction and encouragement. As the mantle of leadership now completely transferred from one man to the other, these words – these final words – are words of blessing and admonition. As we approach the end of our wilderness journey, it is important that we hear and receive these words of instruction as well.

BE STRONG. The Lord God Jehovah is your strength. He is upholding you with His righteous right hand (Isa 41:10). He has armed you with strength for the battle (Psa 18:39). Even in our weakness, His strength is made perfect (2 Cor 12:9). Do not look to your strength; look to His. Do not rely on your ability; rely on His. God will allow you to encounter situations that will test your strength. You will only pass the test as you rely on His strength. His strength is not something you work up to; it is His gift that He freely gives, if we will but submit and ask. Look at Jesus – the first time He came, He did not come as a warrior, He came as a Servant, surrendered and submitted to the Father. And ALL strength and power was given unto Him. Be that surrendered and submitted servant – and as you do, you will be strong.

BE COURAGEOUS. Moses said it here as well, "The LORD goes before you." You are not alone. When i was a young boy, I recall an incident with a bully in our neighborhood that had at least six inches and fifty pounds on me. This kid intimidated the stew out of me. But whenever i was walking in the neighborhood with one of my older brothers, i didn't give this kid a thought. There was no way he would mess with me while i was walking with one of my brothers. i had a courage that came from a confidence in the one with whom i was walking. The same principle applies here. Don't forget with Whom you are walking. There is nothing that you will encounter that He is not able to overcome. The bullies will flee - because they know if they don't, they're going to get a "pounding". Walk with confidence in Him – and as you do, you will be courageous.

DO NOT BE AFRAID. The Lord has promised, *"When you go through deep waters and great trouble, I will be with you. When you go through rivers of difficulty, you will not drown! When you walk through the fire of oppression, you will not be burned up; the flames will not consume you. For I am the LORD, your God, the Holy One of Israel, your Savior. …I love you. Do not be afraid, for I am with you"* (Isa 43:2-5). God does not promise us a journey free of difficulty, but He does promise to walk with us through the difficulty. The only fear that our Lord intends us to have is a healthy fear – a holy reverence and awe – of Him. We are not children of darkness – children of fear – we are children of the Light. Walk boldly in His light – and as you do, you will not be afraid.

DO NOT BE DISCOURAGED. Discouragement arises when, in the midst of difficulty, we take our eyes off of our God and put them on our circumstances. Paul wrote, *"So we don't look at the troubles we can see right now; rather, we look forward to what we have not seen. For the troubles we see will soon be over, but the joys to come will last forever"* (2 Cor 4:18). Our Lord will be with you; "He will neither fail you nor forsake you". The same God who has delivered His people from the bondage of Egypt and has cared for His people through the wilderness will lead His people into His Promised Land. Do not allow the little foxes" that nip at your heels to cause you to become downcast and discouraged. Look up at your Heavenly Father – His Person, His power and His promise – and as you do, you will not be discouraged.

Just as Moses knew the admonition that Joshua was in need of, our Heavenly Father knows even more the words that we are in need of at this stage in our journey. Be strong and courageous; do not be afraid and do not be discouraged. The same God who led you into the wilderness will lead you on and lead you out.

* * *

60

A BLESSING TO HEAR AND TO HEED

"Indeed, You love the people; all Your holy ones are in Your hands. They follow in Your steps and accept Your instruction. ...There is no one like the God of Israel. He rides across the heavens to help you, across the skies in majestic splendor. The eternal God is your refuge, and his everlasting arms are under you. He thrusts out the enemy before you; it is he who cries, 'Destroy them!' So Israel will live in safety, prosperous Jacob in security, in a land of grain and wine, while the heavens drop down dew. How blessed you are, O Israel! Who else is like you, a people saved by the LORD? He is your protecting shield and your triumphant sword! Your enemies will bow low before you, and you will trample on their backs!"
Deuteronomy 33:3, 26-29

* * *

As the people prepared to leave the wilderness to enter the Promised Land, Moses spoke words of blessing over them for one final time. Some of these words applied to all of the people as the children of God, but others applied only to the specific tribe over which they were spoken. In so doing, God was extending a specific promise to each person.

As you have wandered through the wilderness, you have not been alone. God has linked you with others of His children, and in the process He has taught everyone collectively about Himself. He has taught all of us of the promises that are ours as His children, irrespective of who we are. They are promises and blessings that we enjoy as His children by virtue of the relationship that we have with Him through Jesus. God has used this time to bring us to a fresh and greater awareness of His Person, His promises and His purpose. These are "universal" truths that apply to all of us as His children because they are revelations of Who He is and what He has promised. And these have been truths that are best learned through a wilderness journey.

But there are other truths and promises as well. It is true that God's purpose is universal – He is at work to draw all of the peoples of the world to Himself that we might all be reconciled to Him through Jesus; bringing Him the worship, the honor and the glory that He alone is due. But as Dr. Henry Blackaby teaches in *"Experiencing God: Knowing and Doing the Will of God"*, God is always at work around this world to accomplish His purpose. He is pursuing a love relationship with each and every one of us. As we respond to Him, He extends an invitation to each one of us to join with Him in what He is doing. That invitation is personal and specific because the relationship that He desires to have with His children is personal and specific.

For example, as i shared earlier, my wife and i are the proud parents of two teenagers. We love them both equally with our whole heart. As our children, there are rights, honors and blessings that extend to them both, equally because they are our children. But our son and daughter are also as different as night and day. Their passions, their pursuits and their giftedness (all under the lordship of Christ) extend in different directions. God has wired them differently and as such in our role as parents we frequently are coaching them individually in different areas because there are different needs. God is already using them both in a mighty way for His kingdom (and our prayer is that they will stay in that posture of availability to Him and usability by Him); but He is using them in distinctly different ways. Well, such is the case with everyone of us in the body of Christ. And such was the case among the children of Israel; each one uniquely created by the Father for His purpose. Accordingly there are truths and promises that He is revealing to us individually in the wilderness. We all learn differently; and God knows just what we need and just how to teach us. Some things He will teach us collectively; some things will require individual tutoring. Thus the blessings we experience will be both universal as His children and specific as His child.

Moses blessed the people by reminding them of God's unending love for them. He assured them that God would continue to "ride" above, He would continue to undergird them and He would continue to protect them. As they walked with Him, He would enable them to live in safety, enjoying the fruit of the land and the protection of His shield.

But then Moses spoke a word of blessing to each tribe. To the tribe of Reuben – that God give them the tenacity to endure. To the tribe of Judah – that God give them the strength to match their convictions. To the tribe of Levi – that God enable them to rightly teach His Word and His truth, and protect them from the devices of the enemy to distract or detour them from His assignment. To the tribe of Benjamin – Moses reaffirmed the love of God and assured them that they would be preserved from harm. To the tribes of Ephraim and Manasseh, the sons of Joseph – that God bless their land with the finest crops and His conspicuous favor. To the tribe of Zebulun – that God may prosper them as He leads them abroad. To the tribe of Issachar – that God may prosper them at home. To the tribe of Gad – that though they had taken the best land for themselves on the east side of the Jordan, that God may enable their territory to be enlarged. To the tribe of Dan – that God give them the courage of the lion. To the tribe of Naphtali – that they gratefully receive the rich favor and full blessing of the Lord. And lastly, to the tribe of Asher – that God give them the strength to finish well.

God would remind us collectively at this point in our journey of His unending love, His enveloping presence, His certain protection and His bountiful provision. But He would also remind us and bless us individually as we continue on, with His personal blessing – that word aptly spoken just for you. i don't know what that word is that God has for you, but i know that He has it for you. It is His blessing over you. It may not make sense to you today; but the God Who knows your tomorrow has spoken it. He has allowed you to wander in the wilderness so that you might receive it. Hear His blessing over you today; heed it in the days to come and carry it with you.

* * *

61

THE JOURNEY'S END

Then Moses went to Mount Nebo from the plains of Moab and climbed Pisgah Peak, which is across from Jericho. And the LORD showed him the whole land, from Gilead as far as Dan; all the land of Naphtali; the land of Ephraim and Manasseh; all the land of Judah, extending to the Mediterranean Sea; the Negev; the Jordan Valley with Jericho--the city of palms--as far as Zoar. Then the LORD said to Moses, "This is the land I promised on oath to Abraham, Isaac, and Jacob, and I told them I would give it to their descendants. I have now allowed you to see it, but you will not enter the land." So Moses, the servant of the LORD, died there in the land of Moab, just as the LORD had said. He was buried in a valley near Beth-peor in Moab, but to this day no one knows the exact place. Moses was 120 years old when he died, yet his eyesight was clear, and he was as strong as ever. ...There has never been another prophet like Moses, whom the LORD knew face to face.

Deuteronomy 34:1-7, 10

* * *

Two men wandered through the wilderness with the Israelite children; one led them through the wilderness, the other would lead them into the Promised Land. Both had an assignment from God. One was to stop here; the other was to lead the people the rest of the way.

i must confess that on the surface this is one of the most perplexing incidents in Scripture for me. God's hand has been conspicuous on the life of Moses since his birth. God rescued him from the hand of Pharaoh as a little baby in a basket in the bulrushes. God prepared him for his assignment in the walled palace during his first forty years, and then took him to the wilderness pasture to continue his preparation for the next forty years. Then God gave him one of the toughest assignments He has ever given any man – to shepherd His people out of Egypt and to shepherd the Egypt out of His people. For forty years, Moses is the undershepherd of a nation without borders as they migrate through a tract of land small enough to traverse in eleven days. His assignment begins with the intimidation of Pharaoh, the most powerful king on the earth at the time, and continues with the insubordination of the people, some of the most obstinate and ill-natured people you could ever encounter.

God accomplished through Moses some of the greatest miracles that have ever been performed, before or since that time - beginning with the plagues of Egypt and including the parting of the Red Sea, water that poured from rocks and food that came from heaven. God gave him authority over two million plus people, and through him established their form of governance, their military structure and national defense, their manner of worship, their means of conflict resolution and judicial overview, and their constitution – the laws of God. God Himself commends Moses by recording in His Word that there has never been another prophet like Moses; there has never been another man who has known God face to face.

God permitted him to hear and bear the brunt of more murmuring and complaints than any one should have to endure in a lifetime. On more than one occasion the mutinous crowd threatened to stone him. And for 1,262,303,990 seconds he faithfully and obediently followed God. But for 10 seconds at Meribah, he disobeyed God and struck a rock. And i have been struggling with the fact that because of those ten seconds of disobedience, God denied him the opportunity to lead the people into the Promise Land. After all, it wasn't that severe of an action – he struck a rock out of exasperation with the people. If that is Moses' punishment for what he did, i am toast; i have absolutely no chance! But then God prompted me to go back to the burning bush and look at what He had originally told Moses to do. God told Moses to *"lead My people out of Egypt"* (Ex 3:10). Now just before that God had said *"I have come to rescue them from the Egyptians and lead them out of Egypt into their own good and spacious land"* (Ex 3:8). God was going to lead them all the way, but Moses' assignment was to lead them out of Egypt through the wilderness.

. . .

As he climbed Mt. Nebo, Moses had fulfilled his assignment; he had completed the task for which he had been called. And now instead of entering into the reward of the Promised Land, God had something far greater in store. God was allowing Him to enter into the reward of Heaven.

One of the greatest personal experiences the Lord has enabled me to have, has been to stand on the summit of Mt. Nebo – the very place that He led Moses that day. And from that site on a clear day, you can see all of the Promised Land to the Mediterranean Sea to its west; the land that God had promised His servant Abraham. God enabled him to see the land of His promise for the people before He took him home from the wilderness. God's promise for Moses never included the Promised Land. God's assignment for Moses concluded on the eve of its entry.

That realization has caused me to look at the wilderness differently. Too often i make the mistake of looking past the wilderness, trying to see the Promised Land. i become discouraged when all i can see in every direction is wilderness. But what if my assignment is the wilderness? God has told me to go from my Egypt and go to a land that He will show me. What if that land is the wilderness? Will i be content with a promise that stops short of the Promised Land? Will i be content to fulfill my assignment in the wilderness if that is God's plan? We don't get to make the assignments. We're the servants; only the Master gets to make the assignments. Am i willing to follow Him all the way to Mt. Nebo, if that is where my journey is to end? Will i be content to walk according to His plan, even if that walk does not include the Promised Land? It's one thing to be willing to journey through the wilderness; it's quite another to be willing to journey in the wilderness *especially* when you are faced with the possibility that your journey may end there. Am i willing for it to end there, if God so intends?

As we come to the end of this book, our journey together through the wilderness ends here. Some of us are going on into the Promised Land. Some of us are headed to Mt. Nebo. Some of us still have some more wandering to do before our journey in the wilderness concludes. Whatever your status, remember – God led you on this journey. The same God who led you into this wilderness will lead you on and lead you out. But He determines the time and He determines the point of exit, just as He determined the point of entry. Moses trusted Him and experienced Him in ways that no man since has known Him. If you too will trust Him –

completely, no matter where He leads – you too will experience Him in ways that very few ever will.

After all, the lesson of the wilderness is that He alone is God and we are to love Him with our whole heart and soul and mind regardless of the circumstance and regardless of where the journey leads. He wants us to know Him, know Him more and know Him more intimately because He is the God of Heaven and earth, the God of the Promised Land, and yes, even the God of the wilderness!

* * *

PLEASE HELP ME BY LEAVING A REVIEW!

i would be very grateful if you would leave a review of this book. Your feedback will be helpful to me in my future writing endeavors and will also assist others as they consider picking up a copy of the book.

To leave a review, go to:
amazon.com/dp/B010EAR80K

Thanks for your help!

* * *

OTHER BOOKS WRITTEN BY KENNETH A. WINTER

Though the Eyes of a Shepherd

A Novel — **Shimon was a shepherd boy when he first saw the newborn King in a Bethlehem stable.** Join him in his journey as he re-encounters the Lamb of God at the Jordan, and follows the Miracle Worker through the wilderness, the Messiah to the cross, and the Risen Savior from the upper room. Though Shimon is a fictional character, we'll see the pages of the Gospels unfold through his eyes, and **experience a story of redemption – the redemption of a shepherd – and the redemption of each one who chooses to follow the Good Shepherd.**

* * *

Other Books in the *Lessons Learned In The Wilderness* series

Each of the six books in the series contains 61 chapters, which means that the entire series is comprised of 366 chapters — **one chapter for each day of the year.** The chapters have been formatted in a way that you can read one chapter each day or read each book straight through. Whichever way you choose, allow the Master to use the series to encourage and challenge you in the journey that He has designed uniquely for you so that His purpose is fulfilled, and His glory is made known.

The Journey Begins (Book #1)

God's plan for our lives is not static; He is continuously calling us to draw closer, to climb higher and to move further. In that process, He is moving us out of our comfort zone to His land of promise for our lives. That process includes time in the wilderness. Many times it is easier to see the truth that God is teaching us through the lives of others than it is through our own lives.

"The Journey Begins" is the first book in the ***"Lessons Learned In The Wilderness"*** series. It chronicles those stories, those examples and those truths as revealed through the lives and experiences of the Israelites, as recorded in the Book of Exodus in sixty-one bite-sized chapters.

As you read one chapter per day for sixty-one days, we will look at the circumstances, the surroundings and the people in such a way that highlights the similarities to our lives, as we then apply those same truths to our own life journey as the Lord God Jehovah leads us through our own wilderness journey.

Possessing the Promise (Book #3)

The day had finally arrived for the Israelites to possess the land that God had promised. But just like He had taught them lessons throughout their journey in the wilderness, He had more to teach them, as they possessed the promise.

And so it is for us. Possessing the promise doesn't mean the faith adventure has come to a conclusion; rather, in many ways, it has only just begun. Possessing the promise will involve in some respects an even greater dependence upon God and the promise He has given you.

"**Possessing the Promise**" chronicles the stories, experiences and lessons we see recorded in the books of Joshua and Judges in sixty-one "bite-sized" chapters. The book has been formatted for one chapter to be read each day for sixty-one days.

Explore this third book in the "**Lessons Learned In The Wilderness**" series and allow God to use it to teach you how to possess the promise as He leads you in the journey with Him each day.

Walking With The Master (Book #4)

Our daily walk with the Master is never static – it entails moving and growing. Jesus was constantly on the move, carrying out the Father's

work and His will. He was continuously surrendered and submitted to the will of the Father. And if we would walk with Him, we too must walk surrendered and submitted to the Father in our day-to-day lives.

Jesus extended His invitation to us to deny ourselves, take up our cross and follow Him. "**Walking With The Master**" chronicles, through "sixty-one" bite-sized chapters, those lessons the Master would teach us as we walk with Him each day, just as He taught the men and women who walked with Him throughout Galilee, Samaria and Judea as recorded in the Gospel accounts.

The book has been formatted for one chapter to be read each day for sixty-one days. Explore this fourth book in the "**Lessons Learned In The Wilderness**" series and allow the Master to use it to draw you closer to Himself as you walk with Him each day in the journey.

Taking Up The Cross (Book #5)

What does it mean to take up the cross? In this fifth book of the ***Lessons Learned In The Wilderness*** series, we will look at the cross our Lord has set before us as we follow Him. The backdrop for our time is the last forty-seven days of the earthly ministry of Jesus, picking up at His triumphal entry into Jerusalem and continuing to the day He ascended into heaven to sit at the right-hand of the Father.

We will look through the lens of the Gospels at what taking up the cross looked like in His life, and what He has determined it will look like in ours. He doesn't promise that there won't be a cost – there will be! And He doesn't promise that it will be easy – it won't be! But it is the journey He has set before us – a journey that will further His purpose in and through our lives – and a journey that will lead to His glory.

Like the other books in this series, this book has been formatted in a way that you can read one chapter each day, or read it straight through. Whichever way you choose, allow the Master to use it to draw you closer to Him as you walk with Him each day in your journey.

Until He Returns (Book #6)

Moments after Jesus ascended into heaven, two angels delivered this promise: "Someday He will return!" In this sixth and final book of the

Lessons Learned In The Wilderness series, we will look at what that journey will look like ***Until He Returns***. No matter where we are in our journey with Him – in the wilderness, in the promised land, or somewhere in between – He has a purpose and a plan for us.

In this book, we will look through the lens of the Book of Acts at what that journey looked like for those first century followers of Christ. Like us, they weren't perfect. There were times they took their eyes off of Jesus. But despite their imperfections, He used them to turn the world upside down. And His desire is to do the same thing through us. Our journeys will all look different, but He will be with us every step of the way.

Like the first five books in this series, this book has been formatted in a way that you can read one chapter each day or read it straight through. Whichever way you choose, allow the Master to use it to encourage and challenge you in the journey that He has designed uniquely for you so that His purpose is fulfilled, and His glory is made known.

* * *

For more information about these books, including how you can purchase them, go to
wildernesslessons.com or kenwinter.org

WildernessLessons

ABOUT THE AUTHOR

Responding to God's call from the business world in 1992 to full-time vocational ministry, Ken Winter joined the staff of First Baptist Church of West Palm Beach, Florida, serving as the associate pastor of administration and global mission.

In 2004, God led Ken, his wife LaVonne, and their two teenagers on a Genesis 12 journey, that resulted in his serving with the International Mission Board (IMB) of the Southern Baptist Convention. From 2006 until 2015, Ken served as the vice president of church and partner services of IMB, assisting churches across the US in mobilizing their members to make disciples of all peoples.

From 2015 until 2018, Ken served as the senior associate pastor of Grove Avenue Baptist Church in Richmond, Virginia.

Today that Genesis 12 journey continues as Ken labors as a bond-servant of the Lord Jesus Christ in the proclamation of the gospel to the end that every person may be presented complete in Christ.

To read Ken's weekly blog posts go to kenwinter.blog

* * *

And we proclaim Him, admonishing every man and teaching every man with all wisdom, that we may present every man complete in Christ. And for this purpose also I labor, striving according to His power, which mightily works within me.
(Colossians 1:28-29 NASB)

* * *

PLEASE JOIN MY READERS' GROUP

Please join my Readers' Group in order to receive updates and information about future releases, etc.

Also, i will send you a free copy of ***The Journey Begins*** e-book — the first book in the ***Lessons Learned In The Wilderness*** series. It is yours to keep or share with a friend or family member that you think might benefit from it.

It's completely free to sign up. i value your privacy and will not spam you. Also, you can unsubscribe at any time.

Made in the USA
Middletown, DE
17 August 2019